KING'S CROSS KID

VICTOR GREGG was born in London in 1919 and joined the army in 1937, serving first in the Rifle Brigade in Palestine and North Africa, notably at the Battle of Alamein, and then with the Parachute Regiment, at the Battle of Arnhem. As a prisoner of war he survived the bombing of Dresden to be repatriated in 1946, and now lives in Winchester. The story of his adult years, *Rifleman: A Front-line Life from Alamein and Dresden to the Fall of the Berlin Wall*, also co-written with Rick Stroud, was published by Bloomsbury in 2011. An eBook single of his POW experiences, *Dresden: A Survivor's Story*, was published in February 2013.

RICK STROUD is a writer and film director. As well as working with Vic Gregg on *Rifleman* he is the author of *The Book of the Moon* and *The Phantom Army of Alamein: The Men Who Hoodwinked Rommel*. He lives in London.

KING'S CROSS KID

A Childhood Between
the Wars

VICTOR GREGG

with Rick Stroud

BLOOMSBURY
LONDON · NEW DELHI · NEW YORK · SYDNEY

First published in Great Britain 2013
This paperback edition published 2014

Copyright © Victor Gregg 2013
Preface copyright © Rick Stroud 2013

The right of Victor Gregg to be identified as the author of this work has been
asserted by him in accordance with the Copyright, Designs and Patents Act, 1988

Photographs reproduced in this book are from the authors'
own collections except where credited otherwise
Maps by ML Design

Bloomsbury Publishing Plc
50 Bedford Square
London WC1B 3DP

www.bloomsbury.com

Bloomsbury is a trademark of Bloomsbury Publishing Plc

Bloomsbury Publishing, London, New Delhi, New York and Sydney

A CIP catalogue record for this book is available from the British Library

ISBN 978 1 4088 4051 1

10 9 8 7 6 5 4 3 2 1

Typeset by Hewer Text UK Ltd, Edinburgh
Printed and bound in Great Britain by CPI Group (UK) Ltd, Croydon CR0 4YY

I dedicate this book to the memory of my childhood
friends in that long ago time, and especially to the
women who helped me find a pathway through
the years of my youth, now alas all departed.

Those who cannot remember the past are condemned
to repeat it

George Santayana,
The Life of Reason, vol. 1, 1905

CONTENTS

PART TWO

PART THREE

Acknowledgements

Encouragement comes from all points of the compass and in all manner of forms, but reality, in the form of the number of words a publisher might accept, means that only the surface can be skimmed. Right at the top of the pile have to be my editor, Rick Stroud, and his lovely wife, Alexandra, and next to them the young men and women at Bloomsbury, headed by Bill Swainson. There is no doubt in my mind that it has been the persistent encouragement of this small circle that has driven me on. Thanks to them especially, and to Simon Fenwick, archivist to the Shaftesbury Young People Organisation.

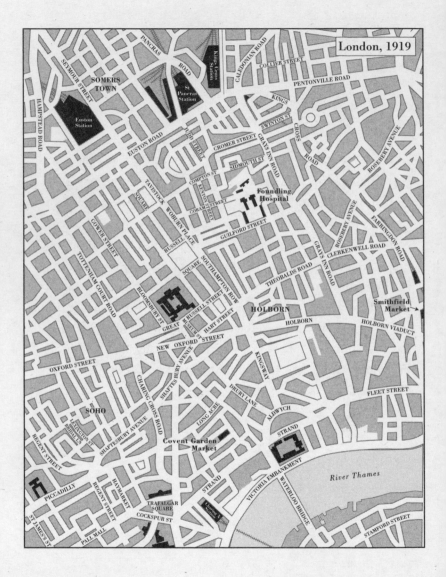

London, 1919

King's Cross and the streets where I was born

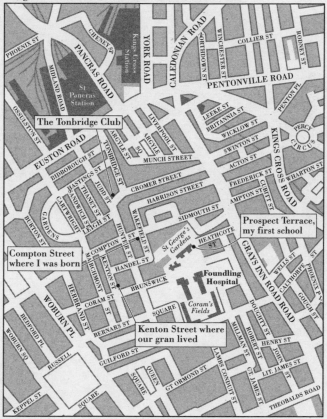

Preface

I first entered the life and world of Victor Gregg in 2009 while researching what life was like for a member of the Rifle Brigade fighting in the Western Desert in the Second World War. I had been given an introduction to Rifleman Gregg by Major Tom Bird who was his company commander in Egypt in 1941. Vic lived in Winchester, home of the Green Jackets and where, in 1937, he started his life as a soldier. When Vic collected me from the railway station that cold autumn day I had no idea that I was meeting an extraordinary man who would later become my friend and co-writer.

That first meeting led to our collaborating on *Rifleman: A Front-line Life from Alamein and Dresden to the Fall of the Berlin Wall*. The title alone gives some idea of the scope of Vic's life and the adventures he's had.

A few months after the publication of *Rifleman*, Vic came up with the idea of writing about his childhood in London's King's Cross between the wars, something he had only briefly touched on in the first book. Vic was born in 1919. His father vanished soon after the birth of Vic's sister, Emily, leaving the children to be brought up by their mother and grandparents. Vic left school when he was fourteen and was soon drawn into the gaudy, violent world of Soho. He was also fascinated by what he calls the 'arty-crafties and beardy-weirdies' of Bloomsbury – the bohemian bunch of artists, writers and political activists. King's Cross, Soho and Bloomsbury are the background to Vic's story.

Vic describes a world that has vanished, swept away by bombing, post-war reconstruction and the welfare state. Just before we were to deliver the manuscript of the book, now entitled *King's Cross Kid*, Vic and I spent one Sunday walking round his childhood haunts. Much more survived than I had expected. While some places had gone completely, the street names were still there, as were many squares, rows of houses and shops.

We walked from the renewed splendours of St Pancras station, where Vic used to steal coal; we had a cup of tea in Exmouth Market, where Vic's first employer owned a sweat shop making spectacle frames; we stood in the doorway of a Peabody Buildings block of flats where the fifteen-year-old Vic knocked a man senseless to defend family honour. What had once been butchers' and greengrocers' shops were almost all now smart coffee houses and restaurants, but, amazingly, the ironmonger where Vic was sent to buy paraffin is not only still there but is owned by the same family and the old, disused gas mantle still hangs from the ceiling.

Slipping in and out of the trendy, well-heeled crowds were the ghosts of eighty years ago: young kids on the scrounge, stealing vegetables from Covent Garden, blagging tips off doormen in the posh hotels. Mothers and fathers desperate, poor, prepared to do anything to feed their children. A mark of that poverty came when Vic said to me, 'You could tell the posh houses round here, they were the ones that had front doors.' Poor as they were, those people had a strong sense of identity and knew how to have a good time and, like Vic, many had a contempt for authority. Their fighting spirit lives on in the pages of this book.

Rick Stroud, October 2012

Part One

I

Morning, King's Cross

I'm lying on a wooden two-tier cot. Down below me, still in the land of nod, my brother John is not yet aware that a new day has dawned. My dad gets up and puts the kettle on for his morning wash and shave, then I can hear my mum getting up. She doesn't get dressed because as soon as my dad is away from the sink her first job is to cook his breakfast. While he shaves I can hear them nattering away to each other. I lie low, because Mum likes us to stay where we are, 'out of harm's way', until she's seen my dad off to work.

After all the clattering and natter between Mum and Dad I peek through the gap in the blankets which hang from a length of sash-cord and divide the family sleeping quarters. I watch Dad pick up his bag of tools, he gives Mum a kiss and off he goes. Silence descends.

'Can we get up now, Mum?' On the way down from my perch on the upper bed I manage to give brother John a sly kick. 'Shall I give 'im a whack, Mum?'

'You dare let me catch you 'itting your little bruvver and I'll tan the arse off yer.'

So I leave John to make himself known in his own time. If he gets up a bit too late then I get first dibs at the porridge our mum puts on the table, and John will be left with the lumpy bits and start howling in protest. Mum might give him a gentle whack to shut him up and I will be smirking all over my face.

2

Four into Two

The four of us live in two pokey little rooms up on the third floor of number nine Compton Street which is in London near King's Cross. The front room faces the street and serves as the family bedroom, lounge and dining room, all in one. The other room is the kitchen and washroom, it is smaller than the front room and looks out on the backyard where all the dustbins and other rubbish are kept. Outside on the landing is the coal box and a big tin bath which hangs from a nail banged into the wall, all nice and handy. There are two toilets in the house, one in the basement that is used by the lady who lives down there, the other on the second-floor landing and for the general use of the rest of the house. Every day the women of the house take turns to keep the toilets, stairs, passages and landings clean. The last thing our dad does before he goes to his bed is to make sure that all the windows are wedged tight with little bits of wood. This is because the slightest breath of wind and everything starts rattling and Dad will wake up grumpy because he couldn't get any sleep. He says the noise reminds him of machine guns going full pelt. I don't know what a machine gun is or what it sounds like and the rattling doesn't keep me awake. The real problem was that our houses were lit by gas and to make the gas burn bright you had to cover the lamp with a mantle, a fragile cotton tube impregnated with some sort of substance that made it glow and stopped it catching fire. The wind can blow in so hard through the gaps in the woodwork that it blows the gas mantle to bits, so Dad has to go outside on to the landing where he keeps a big paraffin lamp with glass all round it that stops the flame from blowing out. Mum says she don't mind the paraffin lamp 'cause she can put her hands over the flame to keep her fingers warm. Our dad gets very angry about what he calls the 'landlord' 'who takes the rent and don't do nothing for it!' Dad says that if he had the chance he'd take this landlord out and shoot him. Mum tells him not to be silly, and then they have a laugh and go to bed. I know all this because I can peek out of the crack in the curtains. Mum and Dad think I'm fast asleep but I'm not.

The lady who lives above us is Mrs Dakin, who Mum calls Elsie. She lives with a black man and Mum says she's Welsh and comes from a place called Cardiff which is a long way away. Elsie is my mum's friend.

3

Prospect Terrace School

In September 1924 I was five and the time had come for me to enrol in the local infants' school. The night before I was due to go Mother pressed my shirt and trousers, made certain that there were no holes in the heels of my socks and cleaned my boots. Our boots always had hobnails hammered into the soles.

In the morning, it was only when we were cleaned and scrubbed and Mum was completely satisfied that we were 'not going to show the family up' that we were allowed to have our breakfast. Mum made us sit up in the correct manner, saying, 'Get yer elbows off the table and sit up properly.' Our breakfast was usually the same every day – a mug of tea and a bowl of Scott's Porridge Oats with a spoonful of Tate & Lyle's Golden Syrup.

Then down into the street with brother John holding tightly on to Mum's arm and off we trot. First into Wakefield Street, then down the slope into St George's Gardens where, ahead of us, stood the imposing red-brick building that was Prospect Terrace School.

Everything about the building had an air of authority. At either end of the roof stood make-believe turrets complete with battlements. I thought the place looked more like a castle under siege than a school. We went in through three stone archways, one for the infants, one for us boys and the third for the girls. The names of each group were carved above the arches, very imposing: INFANTS, BOYS, GIRLS. This building was where I was to start my schooling.

Mum says 'Good morning, God bless' to all the other mothers she knows. On the way to school, we come under the scrutiny of the ever watchful Mr Reid, the chief gardener of St George's Gardens. You can't miss him, always shouting, 'Keep off the grass you lot, what do you think the pathways are for?' Which of course attracts the good-natured jeers of the mums who, true to type, take no notice of any authority.

John was a year younger than me and still clinging to Mum's ankles. She had a folding pram that she used to strap John into. 'Quicker this way,' she used to say, 'can't dawdle around, too much to do.' Mum always seemed to be doing something.

As I walked along beside Mum everything seemed to be right with the world and then, without warning, I was through the arch being shuffled into a line of kids who were complete strangers. Mum had vanished and we were all escorted along a tiled passageway that was the entrance to the infants' school. This was a strange new world and some of the kids began to cry their little eyes out for their mothers.

All of us in the small group of new arrivals were ushered into a large room where there were two ladies dressed in a sort of uniform, all in blue, complete with funny little hats. Then another elderly lady came in and told us that our mums would collect us at the end of the day and that everything was going to be all right. She calmed us down by telling us we were going to have plenty of toys to play with, the usual eyewash. Eventually, after the troubled children had been soothed with the help of a mouthful of sweeties, we were sorted into groups, Red, Blue and Yellow. I don't, today, know which one I was in; it is too long ago and my memory comes back only in fragments. I do sort of recall, or at least have a vague feeling, that along with the rest of the new recruits I didn't really enjoy being parted from my mum and brother John but I don't think I was at all frightened so I must have felt safe in my new world. What I hadn't expected was to be given a hot dinner at midday, including pudding with a helping of custard. The puddings changed according to the day of the week but the custard was a constant and appeared in front of us every day without fail.

That infants' school period lasted for two years, from five to seven, and it was the only time during my schooldays that the sexes were mixed.

The most vivid memory I have of my early years at infants' school is of the time I toppled the treasured maypole that stood in the corner of the main hall. The maypole reached almost to the ceiling and was a very impressive piece of equipment. One day it was dragged into the centre of the hall ready for some event where we were all to dance round it holding on to the long coloured ribbons that hung from its top.

The whole infants' school paraded into the hall, girls in one line, boys in another, and we were each told to hold one of the ribbons, then the girls were to start dancing round the pole, followed by the boys.

One of the teachers sat down at the piano and off went the girls merrily doing their first circuit followed by the boys, including yours truly, who, in a moment of exuberance, gave his ribbon a mighty tug. I was stronger than most of the others and the result was that the maypole started wobbling from the top and slowly the whole contrivance came crashing to the floor, scattering the screaming girls and nearly decapitating the hapless lady at the piano. Luckily for me it never occurred to anyone that the culprit was one of the small innocent looking boys.

I can't remember much from those early years, just flashes, a lot of which are about my dad. Dad never seemed to be part of the household, disappearing before we were out of bed in the morning and reappearing in the evening and then more often than not out again. I never had a clue where he went. I remember the time one day, when school had finished, I was waiting outside looking for Mum and, quite unexpectedly, who turns up but Dad. I was very excited, I jumped up and he put me on his shoulders and carried me sky high. I wanted the world to know that this was my dad.

Another time he came home with a big pile of wood and Mum helped him sort it out. By the time the pair of them had finished, John and I had that big, two-tier bed. Up to then we had been sleeping in our blankets spread out on the floor. That's when Dad strung up the blanket to divide the room.

Another memory which refuses to go away is of Dad lighting up his big paraffin blowlamp. Dad was a plumber and the blowlamp and another tool, a big wrench called 'a pair of stillsons', were the main weapons in his tool bag. The blowlamp served to destroy the armies of bugs, cockroaches and other vermin which infested the tenements and houses where we of the working classes used to live. Dad used to light up this blowtorch and, after giving instructions for us all to stand well clear, would train the flames that came out of the nozzle along the skirting boards, or anywhere else that offered shelter to the tormenting bugs. In those days it didn't matter where you lived – Bermondsey or Bayswater – you had to do battle with the insects that lived in the lath and plaster from which the inside walls of our houses were made.

Every weekend we had the ritual delousing. Mum got us with our heads down over the kitchen table and, using copious measures of carbolic liquid (better known as Condy's fluid), mixed with water and aided by the application of a fine-tooth steel comb, she did her best to rid us of the various types of vermin that bred so freely in our rat hole of a place. It was many years before I realised how hard Mother struggled to keep her offspring fed and looking halfway clean and presentable.

Another memory is of the time Dad took me to a football match. We went along with some of his mates. John wasn't with us because he was too young. After the game we were on the tram, just me and my dad, coming home. He asked me about my friends and I mentioned Freddie Wilson who lived a couple of doors up from us. 'What's he like then?'

'He's my friend.' 'What's 'is mum and dad like?' ''E says 'is dad is always 'itting 'is mum.' Then Dad said to me, very serious, 'Never 'it a woman, son, you can shout at 'em but never 'it 'em, they carn't fight back, you must always love yer mum.' Of all the memories of my dad – and there aren't many of them – that one stays with me.

I can only remember one other instance where he behaved like a dad and that was when he turned up one sunny morning with a motorcycle and sidecar. The sidecar was enormous. Mum and us two boys sat crammed into it while Dad drove us expertly out into the countryside. This episode, more than any other, made my dad seem a real person, a dad like my mates had. These moments were so few and far between in our lives that when Dad finally departed from the scene we boys hardly ever missed him.

He was so tall that when he came into the room everything appeared to be small. Dad's head nearly touched the ceiling and he used to bang his head on the doorway if he ducked a little bit too late.

I have no recollection that we suffered any ill treatment from my dad, neither can I remember there being any violence between him and Mum, so all in all it seems that when I was a little boy life must have been peaceful, happy and content.

One day when the three of us were sitting by the fire, my dad being out, Mum had John on her lap and she told us that Jesus was going to fetch us a little baby and if we were good boys it was possible that Jesus might let us keep the babe for always. This was a shield used by mothers to ward off the possibility of the baby dying at birth, something which often happened.

Our mum talked to us all evening, telling us how good we had to be and saying that as we were big boys now we would have to help her as much as we could. 'Can we take the baby out in the pram, Mum?' (the pram was a fold-up affair hanging on a nail banged into the wall on the landing, the same one in which she sometimes wheeled brother John). 'Let's wait till Jesus brings the baby first and then we can talk about things. Anyway, Granny will be here to help us so off to bed the two of you.' She gave us both a kiss like always and we climbed into our beds. I didn't give brother John a kick this time because I felt good about Jesus and the new babe.

A few days later our grandma from Kenton Street turned up and told me and John that we are going to be sleeping round at her house for the next few days. 'Why's that, Gran?' 'Well, Jesus might be coming with the new baby.' 'Can we see Jesus, Gran?' Gran quickly put us in our place: 'Course not, you're too young to understand these things.' There was never any argy-bargy with our gran, she was terse and to the point. She towered almost menacingly above us two small boys and if there ever was one who had to be obeyed it was our gran. But her stern exterior was only a façade; underneath it all she had a heart of gold and proved it time and time again over the following years.

4

'As Jesus Been Yet?

A few days later, Gran picked us up from school. At home
we found that Mum had been in bed all day. Now I was
sitting by the fire grate watching Gran hustling and bustling
about. She had made brother John go to bed and to keep him
quiet she had bought him a *Tiger Tim* comic, which had plenty
of pictures, which was good because John was too young to
read. All afternoon the room had been full of different people
coming and going. One of them was a big black man who I
found out later was our local doctor. His name was Doctor
Dia and his practice covered the area around Compton, Wakefield, Cromer and the adjoining streets. His surgery was on the
corner of Compton Street and Judd Street and if you had need
to visit him you paid sixpence (if you had it) and sat in the little
parlour-like waiting room until his wife, who was also the
nurse, called out your name. Where he originally came from I
haven't a clue. He was a large man and as black as the ace of
spades and everyone thought the world of him and his wife,
who, by the way, was as white as a stick of chalk.

14

I could see Gran was getting worried; she wanted plenty of pennies for the gas meter and spare gas mantles.

'Where's our dad then, Gran?' 'Never mind about 'im. I've sent 'im back to 'is mother's, carn't 'ave 'im 'ere when Jesus brings the wee babe.'

The next day it was Gran who picked me up again after school and took me to her house in Kenton Street, only about ten minutes' walk away but it could have been in another country. It was situated west of Judd Street, on the posh side. Brother John was already there. After giving us a quick snack of bread and jam and a cup of tea, Gran was off to attend to the needs of her only daughter.

Before she went she gave us our orders: 'Behave yerselves and get up to no mischief, I'll be back in an hour to get yer granddad's dinner. If yer make the place untidy I'll give yer both a thump', and then she was gone. As soon as we were alone John started to crawl all round the kitchen, upsetting Gran's pots and pans which she kept under the shelf of what she called her Welsh dresser. We spent the next hour trying to put everything back in place but we didn't succeed. When Gran got back she forgot about the thump and instead gave us both a big kiss and a hug. We thought our mum and gran were the best people in the whole world. We were both full of excitement about the promise of the new baby. ''As Jesus been yet, Gran?' 'No, Victor, probably tonight and we think you might be getting a little baby sister.' I didn't think much of the arrival of a sister: 'Girls are always crying, Gran, carn't I 'ave anuvver bruvver?' 'Don't be wicked, Victor, you get what God gives you and don't forget to say your prayers before you go to sleep tonight, ask God to look after your mummy.' 'Yes, Gran, I promise.' 'You're both going to sleep on the floor upstairs, if you make any noise Granddad will come up and give you both a thump.' With that ultimatum delivered she started to collect the things she thought she might need, then took us both up to the front room and, after reminding us about our prayers, left us to our thoughts and the darkness of a strange room. Brother John, who had been taught to learn his evening prayers by rote, put his hands together and started saying 'Our Father', but he had forgotten how it went and jumbled up the words.

5

Little Emmy

The arrival of sister Emily changed our lives completely. One morning, less than a month after she was born, Dad went to work and that was the last we ever set eyes on him. It was as quick and abrupt as that: he just jumped ship and vanished into thin air. Gran came round our house every day for weeks, comforting and consoling her daughter. Notices were put in the paper, Gran went to the Salvation Army who were reckoned to be good at finding errant fathers, but the weeks turned into months, and eventually Mum stemmed her tears. After Dad disappeared John and I hardly missed him, but we felt our mum's pain and that made us sad. Mother, who had been trained as a milliner, managed to get some home work from a firm in Bridle Lane, up near Leicester Square. Granddad came up with a second-hand Singer treadle sewing machine and our front room was turned into a bedroom-cum-dining room-cum-nursery-cum-workshop all in one. John still had six months to go before he was due to start at the infants' school, and little

Emily just lay in the top drawer of a chest of drawers that served as a cot and burbled happily away. I knew Mum was hurt, and hurt very deeply, but she seemed happy enough singing away in time with the treadling whatever gospel song came to her mind.

Every week Mother visited the relief centre, a council building that stood at the lower end of Great College Street. It was the distribution point where the women of the area gathered to plead for and collect their weekly ration of food coupons which could be exchanged at specially designated shops. We called it the 'Poor House'. My memories of those humiliating visits will remain with me for ever, standing beside my mum, clutching on to her trembling hand while she faced the local council's poor relief officials, three of them, a man and two unfriendly looking women. I have had problems with authority ever since.

Once I was with my mum sitting down with all the other women when her name was called out. She grabbed my hand and we stood in front of these grown-ups who were going to give my mum her food tickets. The woman sitting behind the table said something to my mum that made her burst into tears, and as she let go of my hand to wipe her eyes I dashed up to the platform and kicked the woman who had made my mum cry. 'You're a witch, you made my mum cry, I know what a witch is, you're a witch.' I was told that I was shouting and screaming fit to wake the dead. But I was also told that Mum got the extra coupons she had pleaded for.

On the walk home Mum collected what food we needed for the next three or four days. She always included a tin of

Tate & Lyle's Golden Syrup as a special treat for us boys. As well as having it on our morning porridge (which she was a great believer in), it also livened up the dryness of the stale loaves of bread. The only time John and I ever tasted fresh bread was when we were round at Gran's in Kenton Street. Stale loaves only cost a penny whereas a fresh loaf was three-pence and sometimes even more.

When Granddad learnt of my fracas with the relief people he patted me on the back and gave me twopence to buy some sweets. Gran wasn't so sure: 'Don't encourage 'im to be rude to 'is betters, Will, he's too cheeky for 'is age as it is.' I still got the twopence.

After little Emily had been with us for six months or more Mum got a permanent job with the firm in Bridle Lane which meant she was a bit better off and we could afford to buy fresh bread instead of the stale bread and, more impor-tantly, she didn't have to go begging any more.

One evening we were round our gran's in Kenton Street where our mum used to pick us up on her way home from work. 'Gran, can we take the babe round the block in the pram? It's nice and sunny out.' Gran wasn't too sure about this. She was frightened of us larking about and tipping the pram over. 'We'll be very careful, Gran.' It worked. Gran tucked little Emily into the pram, making certain that all the straps were tight, and we set off. 'Where we going then?' says John. 'I thought we could go and meet Mum from work.' 'That's miles away,' he moaned. 'No it ain't, twenty minutes that's all, we can take the babe for a nice ride and Mum can show her to her friends.' 'Gran will give us a thump when we get back.' 'Nah she won't, we're giving her a rest.' Soon we were in Soho, almost at Bridle Lane, and pushing our way through the people who were rushing out of their offices and shops on the start of their journey home. In Lexington Street, where our Uncle Frank worked, a big policeman appeared in front of us. 'Where do you think you two are going with that baby, and where did you find it?' It didn't take long for a crowd to gather to get a better view of the two scruffs who had nicked some poor mother's child. The copper bent down to get a look at our Emmy who, because the pram had come to a stop, was beginning to bawl her little head off. 'You keep yer 'ands off our Emmy,' I scream at the copper. By this time John was near to tears, but he turned the situation: 'We're going to meet our mum from work, Emmy is our baby sister.' The policeman had now switched his attention away from me and was listening to John, who could make people think that butter wouldn't melt in his mouth. The policeman stood aside, the crowd dispersed and we continued the last couple of hundred yards to where Mum worked.

As soon as we got there down came the girls, saying their goodnights and full of the chatter that women are so good at. We both spotted Mum at the same time and in seconds we were surrounded by her friends who all wanted to have a go at holding Emmy. I could see that Mum was very happy showing her baby around, then I saw the copper who was still hanging around. 'Look, Mum, 'e wanted to pinch our Emmy. 'E was going to lock us up in the cop shop.' In a few seconds the women's attention had been diverted from little Emmy to the large figure of the policeman. 'You ought to be ashamed of yerself. Fancy frightening little boys. Go and fight someone yer own size.' All the women let the copper have it without mercy. In the end he made the best of the situation and slunk away.

John was still worried about getting a thump from Gran when we got home, but Mum said, 'Don't be silly, John. Granny won't hurt yer, mind yer, she might tell yer both off, quite right too.'

Together John and I used to have a lot of fun pushing little Emmy around in the pram, which to us was nothing more than an outsize toy. Luckily Emmy never suffered any injuries from our many escapades.

6

Losing My Marbles

I was now nearly seven and becoming aware of life outside of the walls of our house. The kids from Wakefield Street played together, likewise the kids from other streets, and as a natural course of events I drifted towards the street nearest to our house, Wakefield Street. The boys I spent my time playing with became my companions for the next ten years.

My first insight into the power of property came when I was standing alone in the playground watching some of the Wakefield kids playing marbles.

Playing marbles was less important than owning a bigger bag of marbles than anyone else. In the game you aimed your own marble at your opponent's and, if you hit one, that marble became yours. Arguments arose in the wink of an eye; no marble was handed over without resort to a show of fists. I knew that I had to get my hands on some marbles as soon as possible. That evening I asked my mum if I could have a penny to spend. 'What for?' 'I want to buy some marbles, Mum.' 'Well, yer won't get many for a penny', and she gave me twopence.

The next morning before school started I went to the sweetshop next to the school where you could buy marbles of every kind, from the cheap clay coloured ones to the more popular glass 'glarnys' and the grand, ornamental glass 'Wizards'. The clay marbles sold for about ten for a penny while the real posh ones cost as much as sixpence each. Once acquired, the marbles became a source of riches. If you owned a bag of fifty marbles you could barter them for almost anything; all that was necessary was the initial stake and the ability to get your hands on as many of the other kids' marbles as you could without losing any of your own.

After a couple of weeks I was the proud possessor of a collection of more than two hundred which I used to take home, and with Mum's help count them over and over again.

By now I had the full backing of the Wakefield Street kids, but had aroused the envy of the Harrison Street lot who challenged us to a game. The game took place in the play-ground of the infants' school; the average age of the combatants was about seven and as far as I can remember there were about fifteen of us. The game ended in a glorious punch-up, after which all the marbles of both sides were confiscated. The head teacher lined us up, read the riot act, told us to hold out our hands and then belted each one of us with a wooden ruler. That finished me with marbles. There had to be other ways to get rich.

John was now at the infants', too, and when Gran came round to collect us she had to endure a full account of the marbles incident and her grandson's addiction to violence in the playground. I remember Gran told the teacher that unless she held her tongue when speaking about Victor, who never did anything wrong, she would feel the back of my gran's hand. Luckily for me Gran failed to tell Granddad what had happened; he had a very heavy hand and believed strongly in the saying 'spare the rod and spoil the child'.

7

Big Boys Don't Cry

One evening sometime around July, we were all sitting near the window, little Emily safely ensconced on our mum's lap, when the bell rang out on the landing and we heard the sound of several pairs of footsteps climbing the stairs. The door was wide open so there was no need to knock. The next thing our mum was greeting the local rep from the Salvation Army. He was dressed up in his uniform complete with cap and gold braid and accompanied by a young lady in a similar uniform, and another couple in ordinary clothes. The room was full to bursting. John and I sat on the floor ogling these strange people who had suddenly come into our lives. My mum had to answer some questions and I was sure that I spied little tears in her eyes. Then, as suddenly as they came they said their farewells and promised Mum 'not to worry, everything will turn out for the best'. Next day Gran announced that Victor was to be going on a holiday, starting with a train ride with her and Uncle Joe.

What had really happened was that my mother, at her wits'
end as to how to cope, had turned to the Salvation Army
who had advised her to send me, her eldest, to a home for
destitute boys. And so it was that I landed up in one of what
were called Shaftesbury Homes.

I left home on a train accompanied by Uncle Joe and my
gran. I held her hand for the whole trip; she probably thought
she would never see her grandson again. Uncle Joe kept up a
non-stop patter, trying to keep me occupied, but neither of
them seemed to be very happy.

I discovered later that Joe was Granddad's brother and lived
in the buildings off Rosebery Avenue, just down the road.
Gran had probably got on to Joe and insisted that he escort
her to give her a bit of moral support. There was little finesse
about the handover. No doubt the staff at the home were
used to the sight of grieving mothers handing over their
beloved offspring.

In no time at all my gran and Uncle Joe were bundled into
a waiting horse-drawn carriage – perhaps it was an ambulance, I don't really know – and in spite of all the years that
have gone by since they left me at the home I can still bring
back the loneliness I felt after the two of them had been
swept out of the grounds and slowly disappeared from view.
The staff, for whom all this must have been familiar, kept me
busy, showed me around and kept me occupied. I had entered
a new world, a world of light and open spaces, and yet I felt
completely lost.

The house was surrounded by green fields and trees, and it
had high rooms with huge windows that reached from the

floor to the ceiling and highly polished wooden floors. I soon discovered just how much work went into keeping those floors in that high-gloss state.

I was part of a new intake and we were escorted to a room that was painted all white. Sitting at a desk in the centre of the room was a lady in a dark-blue dress with a funny hat to go with it. She told us to address her as 'Matron' and that it was her job to make certain that we kept ourselves clean. 'Right, boys, get in line, and strip off those dirty clothes.' 'Wot, everyfing, miss?' 'Don't let me hear any of you call me "miss" again, you address me as Matron, yes, everything.' Then she rang the bell on her desk and a man in a white coat came in. He examined our hair and fingernails before telling us to bend over, whereupon there was a further examination.

Then another boy was called who issued us each with a towel and a small bar of soap, then led us into another room where we all stood in line waiting for this man to chop our hair off. We all finished up in the washroom under the showers. They were freezing. The torture only came to an end when we were issued with our new clothing which was a sort of uniform: denim trousers and jackets and a couple of shirts made of the same material. These were called work clothes. There was always two of everything, one on and one in the wash. Then we had a navy-blue coat, shirt and trousers, which were meant to be worn on church parades, which took place twice a week, once in the morning and once in the evening on Sundays. There were also two pairs of socks which were grey wool with a coloured band at the top. These were worn pulled up as far as possible with the tops neatly folded over with the coloured bands level on both legs. Finally, I was issued with a cap for everyday wear, close-fitting with a peak.

Then all the new boys lined up, and by now we didn't know if we were coming or going. Our names were read out along with the name of the house we were being assigned to.

The Shaftesbury was divided by age. The first group was boys like me aged between six and nine, the next group was for the nine- to eleven-year-olds and finally the eleven- to fourteen-year-olds. At the age of fourteen most of the boys were sent to join the dormitories of British naval establishments like Devonport.

Some of the bigger boys were called prefects and one of these had the job of walking up and down the corridors at first light clanging away with a big brass hand bell until all the boys were out of their beds and waiting to be marched to the wash-houses, where a gang of the prefects waited to see that every boy carried out his ablutions to the letter.

Each boy had his own washing kit and it was impressed upon us that the most important piece of the kit was the toothbrush, which was made of wood with hard black bristles sticking out on the end. We were each issued with a measured amount of white powder which we kept in a special tin. What the powder consisted of is anyone's guess but it certainly kept our teeth shiny white.

After we had washed, the prefects marched us back to the dormitories where we had to make our beds, folding the blankets and sheets and piling them on the end of the bed with our washing kit all neatly laid out. The unfortunate boys who were bed-wetters had to put all their sheets and anything else that might have got wet into a big storage bin. When we went back to the dormitories after breakfast they found a fresh issue had been placed upon their beds.

Next in the day we were marched from the dormitory to the dining room where the first thing was prayers and a morning hymn. Then we had 'morning orders' which were read out by one of the teachers who told us of anything out of the ordinary that was scheduled for the day. Finally, we had to sing the school hymn and then the teacher who had led the singing signalled to us all to sit down and the kitchen staff at last presented us with whatever evil concoction they had dreamed up in the early hours. This was nearly always a bowl of porridge, salted not sweetened, then we had a boiled egg or a kipper.

We all liked the kippers the best; the eggs usually turned out to be rock-hard and, of course, the porridge wasn't nearly as good as our mum's. Bread, already spread with margarine, was doled out from large tureens. On Sundays, as a special treat we got small pots of marmalade to spread on the bread.

To us boys that breakfast consisted of more edible food in one meal than we were used to in a single day at home. And as a bonus we got hot food on the table three times a day, breakfast, dinner and the evening supper. And for the first time in my young life I was wearing clothes that hadn't been patched up and darned.

After breakfast we were marched from the dining hall back to the dormitories.

On the first morning those boys who had come into the home on the same day as myself were taught the mysteries of 'getting dressed in a proper manner'.

Then it was off to the classroom, just like school at home except in this place the teachers didn't walk about with a cane permanently at the ready. Everything in the Shaftesbury Home seemed to me quieter and more ordered than the schooling I had been used to.

If someone broke the rules, the offender was paraded before the rest of the boys as a sort of traitor to the good name of the class. But instead of the boy being punished, the whole class had some of its privileges withdrawn. This was really clever stuff and much more effective than the canings I was used to.

Like the rooms in the rest of the institution the classrooms were huge, high and wide. The lessons concentrated on the importance of the British Empire, big maps of which hung from the walls. Where there was available space between the maps, pictures of huge sailing ships were hung, or, in the jargon of the school, British men o' war.

We were taught to feel proud of being part of the biggest empire in the world, and were drilled to remember the important days like Trafalgar Day, Empire Day, the King's Birthday. I remember that on one of these great anniversaries a band arrived and we spent the day marching up and down, bugles blowing. Different flags were hoisted on the big flag pole that stood in the centre of the parade ground. I can't remember what day we were celebrating but I do remember the noise and excitement and the grand carry-on.

At first I thought I was on some form of strange holiday; it never crossed my mind that it might be a permanent arrangement. But, as the days passed and the holiday did not come to an end I began to feel more and more depressed. I was in a sort of limbo and I found that very hard.

After a few days I was taken up to a room by one of the prefects who knocked on the door and a voice called 'Come in'. Inside was an old man with long grey hair. He told me to sit down beside him and told the prefect that he could go. He offered me a large saucer of sweets and said: 'Have a sweetie, Victor, nobody here is going to bite you.' Then he told me that it had been reported to him that I appeared to be very unhappy and he asked if I understood why I was there. I was only seven and was now a bit frightened. I did not know how to answer, but I tried. 'My gran said I was going on a holiday. When can I go home to my mum?' This was one of the few times that I shed tears. 'Dry your eyes, Victor, big boys don't cry and you are a big boy now, aren't you?' He said this in such a way that I had no option but to nod my head. Then he offered me another sweet and explained why it had been necessary to take me in, how hard it was for my mother. He said he was certain that everyone at home loved me very much and if I needed to talk to someone I only had to ask one of the teachers. He gave me no indication of how long I might stay but I must have felt a lot better after the interview as I apparently knuckled down and got into the swing of things. So much so that after some weeks I was again taken to the office and presented with a star that I was told to sew on to my going-out shirt. I remember being very proud of the star although I never understood what it stood for.

When the weather was fine the prefects took us outside to show us how to march in lines four abreast swinging our

arms level with our shoulders. On rainy days, instead of the
marching drill the class was taken to the gym, a huge hall
with all manner of equipment, including vaulting horses
which we were encouraged to run at and somehow leap
right over. Not many of my class could get anywhere near
jumping them, but the teacher who led us was quite a jolly
sort of man, always laughing and joking. I know that I looked
forward to these gym periods.

I wanted to prove to the others that where I came from the
boys were braver than anybody else. Hanging from the ceiling on the end of these thick ropes were big iron rings
covered in leather. I discovered that when I stood on one of
the benches the rings came down to within an inch of the
top of my head.

A couple of weeks later, back in the gym, I decided that
now was the chance to prove that I was not to be messed
with. I shouted to the boys, 'Oy, you lot, watch this.' Then I
dragged a bench under one of the rings, stood on it, grabbed
the ring which seemed to weigh a ton, and swung it as hard
as I could towards the ceiling. Up it went . . . and down it
came like a thunderbolt. It didn't stop an inch above my head
but bounced squarely off my forehead and knocked me cold.

I came to in the matron's room with a bandage round my
head and a massive bruise and swelling. As soon as I had
regained consciousness, Matron called the headmaster and I
was grilled as to why I had behaved in such an irresponsible
manner, told how lucky I was to be alive, and that if anything
had happened to me I would have brought disgrace to the
school. I found out afterwards that the reason things had

gone so wrong was because the benches were different heights. I had picked a bench that was higher than the one I had originally stood on, hence the whack. Instead of impressing the rest of the boys with my daredevil stunt I was now looked upon as something of a nutcase.

Another piece of training gear which we were all encouraged to become good on was a structure in the shape of a ship's mast complete with crossbars and rope ladders. We were taught to shin up the ladders, walk along the crossbars and then take up positions where we could work on imaginary sails. Each boy had a rope harness attached to his body, but as soon as a boy could climb without the safety harness he was awarded a badge with a picture of the mast on it, which he had to sew on to his best church parade uniform. I was in the youngest class so we were only allowed to climb up to the first beam, but we thought it was very high. I never heard of any boy falling off though.

Another sport we did was boxing. There was a full-size ring in the corner of the gymnasium. The same master who trained us on the vaulting horse taught us to box, how to keep our guard up, how to put the full weight of the body behind the shoulder when aiming a punch, that sort of thing. He drilled it into us that it was no use getting into the ring unless you intended to hurt someone. During my stay at the home I took some painful knocks. The sports teacher never let things get out of hand, and I used to enjoy those sessions in the ring even when I came off second best.

Once two of the boys did something wrong (I don't remember what), and we were told that we could not go to the gym. Instead we would polish the floors. We were all marched down to the cellars where the caretaker issued us with huge, heavy 'bumpers', iron plates with stout handles to which a polishing cloth was fixed. The rest of the boys got on their hands and knees to apply the wax polish. Those with the bumpers pushed them up and down, buffing the boards. The exercise ended when the prefects deemed that the floor had the necessary shine from corner to corner. Then we marched off to the showers to clean off all the sweat and grime accumulated in the exercise. I was surprised the boys took all this without a murmur of dissent; back home at school at Prospect Terrace there would have been a whole-sale bundle.

After I had been there some few weeks I and some of the other boys were paraded in the main hall and told that we were to be moved to the next class. To mark this new status we were to be issued with new hats, to be worn whenever we were outside the walls of the school. These turned out to be like the hats worn by the sailors of the Royal Navy – 'and always to be worn straight across the forehead with the bow of the ribbon dead centre at the rear of the head'.

Once we had this new 'outside gear', the class was allowed to take part in the weekly Sunday morning march to the local church. To attend the service we formed up in columns of four, about fifty or sixty boys, with the prefects marching outside the ranks shouting 'left, right, left, right'. All us boys enjoyed playing at soldiers and we made sure our hats were on dead straight. It must have been a fair-sized town as I remember that we had some competition from the local

Scout Group and a company of the Boys' Brigade who had a band and so always led the parade. I was already familiar with the Boys' Brigade as they had a company in Wakefield Street back home. Seeing them next to me on those Sundays got me to thinking about my mum and John and little Emmy. It made me very unhappy.

Sunday afternoon was visiting day and the boys used to gather at the windows waiting to see if their parents were going to appear with a bag of goodies. If the day was fine they waited at the gates. It doesn't need a big brain to imagine the sense of loneliness when the visitors failed to appear, which often happened, because it was impossible for most of the families to afford the fare to travel to and from the home.

Although I missed my mum, at the same time I felt a strange sense of security and wellbeing. Then, one day, I was called to the front of the class and told to report to the headmaster's room. One of the older boys escorted me to his office and left me alone there, wondering what fate had in store for me. The head came in and told me that the next morning I had to hand in all my washing and cleaning kit because my parents were coming to collect me. As a parting shot he said: 'We're sorry to lose you, Victor. We think you would have been a pride to the British navy.' That's what the man said. I remember it as if it was yesterday.

The next morning everything carried on as normal – up, wash, breakfast, into the first class of the day, and then the second, and on into the dining room for lunch. By now I was almost in tears; my mum wasn't coming after all. Finally, I was marched into the headmaster's office where I found my gran and the ever faithful Uncle Joe sitting down, finishing some refreshments that the head had laid on.

The head told me to go to Matron and put on the clothes I'd arrived in, which were all done up in a parcel. No matter how hard I tried, none of the clothes would fit me, they were all too small and tight. Eventually it was decided that I should keep the clothes I was wearing, all except the hats. My gran was pleased about my sailor's outfit as it saved having to buy me new clothes.

I remember being reunited with Mum. She was crying and laughing at the same time, hugging me to her and showing the love that only a mother can give. Later in life I learnt that my going away had driven Mum into a complete mental breakdown. Gran decided that things had gone too far and that she had to get me back. She and Granddad decided that they would have brother John to live with them, which took a load off my mum's shoulders. When I arrived home and John was no longer there, the place seemed empty. My stay at the Shaftesbury Home was history. Mother never mentioned it and I sensed the hurt it must have caused her, and never raised the subject myself.

8

Mean Streets

My time away from home must have done me some good. I had grown skywards and Mother decided that I was getting too big to sleep in the same room with two women, so she decided to move my bed into the kitchen. It finished up in a space between the gas cooker and the kitchen sink and, despite all Mum's efforts to keep the place clean, as soon as darkness fell a cracking and rustling announced the arrival of an advance guard of cockroaches and our resident family of mice. Mother had a way of her own as far as the mice were concerned. She used to set a bucket half filled with water in the centre of the room. Then she fixed up a small length of wood to the side of the bucket, like a child's seesaw. On the end of the strip of wood she put a lump of evil-smelling cheese. The unsuspecting rodents smelt the cheese and ran along the piece of wood, causing the wood to dip down, flinging the mouse and any of his mates who were with him into the water. Sometimes a dozen or so of the mice finished up in this watery grave. In the morning the bucket went straight down the toilet, and a good flush made sure we were mouse-free for at least a couple of days.

We soon got back into a routine. After breakfast Mum took Emmy off to our gran's, then went on her way to work leaving me to find my own way to school. All except Wednesday mornings when it was my job to take the 'bag wash' round to the Sunlight laundry. This meant cramming all our dirty clothes into a large canvas bag which was held closed with a big brass clasp complete with padlock. Each clasp had a number stamped into it as a means of identification. I had to struggle round to Cromer Street with it and then, after school on Thursday, collect the finished wash. The bag was big and heavy and I could only just manage it but I knew that I was saving our mum a lot of work.

While I was at the home I had been upgraded to the boys' school and brother John had been moved to a small infants' school in Herbrand Street, much nearer to my gran in Kenton Street. Losing John affected me more than I expected: now I had no one to play with or take the mickey out of during the long winter nights. To our mum it was a life-saver, but to me our home had lost something. The saving grace was, being just over seven years old, I was now expected to find my amusements outside the walls of our home. This meant that I was beginning to mix full-time with the kids I went to school with.

Although the walk to school only involved a stroll of about half a mile I soon learnt that even that short distance was fraught with danger. The school served three streets and each had enough young boys to constitute a medium-sized gang

– Sidmouth Street, Harrison Street and our smaller Wakefield Street.

The Sidmouth Street lot were more vicious than the other two, and it was reckoned that they were the top dogs. Their street was right next to the school. The Wakefield and Harrison Street gangs had to walk together and sort out their differences as they went along. If a dispute arose in the morning and wasn't settled by school time it would fire up on the short walk home, much to the annoyance of those mums who were still collecting their young from the infants' school. Mr Reid the gardener used to set about us with a big broom made from the branches of trees. The boys met up in the evening and spent their time working out who had bashed who and looking forward to the next encounter. I had other problems. The semi-naval uniform that the home had provided me with, although much warmer and more comfortable than my old clothes, marked me out as different from all the other boys. While the other mums remarked how smart I looked, I had to suffer non-stop jeering and catcalls. 'Oi tosher, where's yer boat?' was the most common. But I was big for my age and the food and the exercise had developed my body, so anyone taking the mickey had to risk having a fight with me. In time, as my clothes got scruffier, I became less and less a target and more one of the gang.

At Prospect Terrace School the young girls aged between seven and eleven helped cook the school meals as part of their curriculum; they were also taught the arts of knitting and darning. After all, that's what girls did. The meals cost twopence per child but even that was too much for some parents so the dining room was never overcrowded.

If you looked into the playground you could see the difference between the girls and the boys. The girls would be skipping or playing hopscotch, with much screaming and laughing and playing around. A playful, happy scene.

Not so the boys. By the time we were seven the gangs started to form. The boy with the best fighting ability would be the gang leader and any attempt to displace him could only be achieved by a bundle. These confrontations usually took place in a corner of the playground. The teachers seldom interfered unless it was obvious that real injury was on the cards; a loose tooth or a bloody nose was not considered to be anything to bother the headmaster with, and the boy who came out worse in the argument had the sense to accept the fact that he wasn't leadership quality yet.

When the mother turned up at the school to collect her offspring, and she saw little Johnny with a bruised face and perhaps a torn jacket, she'd cuff him smartly round the ears, saying, 'If I catch you fighting again, I'll tell your dad.' The dad's attitude was usually, 'If you're going to fight, hit 'em 'ard and don't come crying to me.' Boys were raised to look after themselves.

It was the same outside school. The boys had their own corner of the street, to which they returned after they'd been roving about engaged in some mischief or trespassing on a weaker gang's domain. The girls likewise commandeered a section of the street where they could play out their fantasies, such as pretending to be film stars or maybe a princess looking for a handsome prince. The 'handsome prince' was usually one of the boys in the street's gang. The girls all knew who fancied who, but the boys on the other hand looked upon the girls as an oddity that had to be tolerated. Even so the boys always regarded the girls as their property and any attempt by boys of another street to interfere with or annoy what they called 'their girls' always resulted in a bout of serious fighting. Kids from the same street regarded each other as brothers and sisters, all part of a family. Streets were sacrosanct to the people who lived in them. Three or more boys entering a strange street immediately became subjects of suspicion and more often than not they were challenged.

I remember a typical event in the King's Cross area in the early 1930s. A bunch of six or seven of the young boys in the Harrison Street gang, aged anything between eight and eleven, had got bored with kicking their rag ball up and down the road and somebody suggested that it might be a good thing to go and annoy the Wakefield Street gang, just around the corner,

'Let's go and bash 'em up.' With no further ado off they set, singing and shouting, dragging sticks against the railings, letting everybody know that the Harrison Street gang were on the march.

The boys of the Wakefield Street gang were engrossed in a game of cricket, with a piece of wood shaped like a cricket bat and a hard rubber ball. A few minutes earlier the ball had smashed through one of the upstairs windows of a nearby building. The players were debating whether to scarper or to dare to ask for their ball back.

The boys from Harrison Street arrived and one of them pushed his way into the bunch, addressing one of the smaller members of the Wakefield Street lot: 'Oi, four-eyes, gis that bat.' The boy in question, the owner of the spectacles, replied by lifting the bat and swiping the intruder around the head, drawing blood. This was a sudden and unexpected defence of property and the lad who had demanded the bat was now howling his head off, blood streaming from his mouth as a result of the teeth that had been smashed by the blow.

The leader of the Harrison Street gang now made his presence felt. He approached the eldest and biggest of the Wakefield lot: 'Oo you looking at then, tosher?' – this was the normal form of address that signified that a bundle was in the offing – 'I fink I'm looking at a load of turd.' This question and answer session would go on until one of the boys struck the first blow, which meant the start of an all-out fight between the two opposing forces. But the leader of the Harrison Street gang broke the unwritten code of the streets: never make remarks about someone's mother. 'You ain't got a farver, 'ave yer?' 'What's it to you?' 'You're a barsterd, ain't yer?' 'What yer mean by that?' 'Your mum's had a barsterd!!!' Without further ado the boy without a father hurled himself at his adversary, giving no quarter, tearing the other boy's face to ribbons. The brawl came to a sudden halt when one of the boys shouted: 'Look out, the rozzers are here.' Quick as lightning, the street cleared of the boys of both sides, all except the one who had dished out the last lot of damage.

The burly policeman, who was nicknamed 'the Bear' because of his massive girth, called the boy over, and when he came close bent down, the better to bring himself to the boy's size. 'He ain't gonna talk like that about your mum again, is he?' The Bear was reckoned by one and all as some-one not to mess with. 'You gonna take me round the cop shop then?' said the boy, probably thinking that to show some form of defiance might be to his good. 'Not this time, sonny boy, I saw what happened, but a warning in your little ear, don't get cheeky with me, and always show respect for the law. Now shove off and behave yourself.'

Later that evening, the plates had been cleared away and little Emmy was asleep in her rough cot, while Mother was stitching some work she had brought home in order to earn a bit extra. Suddenly I said, 'Mum, is Farver ever going to come home?' Mum looked at me, 'Why do you ask that, Victor?' 'No reason, Mum, I was just finking.' Mother put down her work and without warning tears started rolling down her face. I felt guilty that I had made her cry. I put my arms round her and said: 'Don't cry, Mum, I didn't mean to make you cry, we will always look after you when we grow up.' Mum wiped her eyes and stood up: 'Come on, Victor, off to bed with you. And, by the way, Mrs Brown next door told me about the happenings of today. Fighting is never a good way to settle an argument.' This from a woman who had lost two of her brothers in the senseless slaughter of the Great War.

9

Harsh Lessons

Life in the junior boys' school was harsh, and the slightest deviation from the straight and narrow was severely punished. And in some ways it had to be. Any sign of weakness or hesitation on the part of the teacher would be picked up by the quick-witted assortment of young scruffs sitting in front of him. Our teachers were always men. Discipline was enforced by a swipe with the cane which all teachers carried, and a boy could be caned severely for the slightest misdemeanour. Neither the boys nor their parents thought it necessary to challenge the authority of the school; it was accepted that if the boy had done wrong he had to take his medicine. Yelling while the cane or strap was doing its worst was allowed, crying wasn't, and if you were silly enough to complain to your father, or in my case my mother, you got another whack for good measure.

One of the boys in our class was a real basher; his mum and dad were reckoned to be people who started a fight if they could find no better way of amusing themselves. On

44

one occasion the boy shouted at his teacher and told him he didn't give a f— about ''im and 'is cane', whereupon the said teacher lost his cool and laid into the kid. The boy retreated under the weight of blows and ran out of the class heading for the safety of his mum's arms.

We all knew what was going to happen to the teacher once the mum found out. Sure enough, late in the afternoon the whole school heard the sound of the boy's mother screaming her head off, pulling her son by the collar of his shirt into the classroom. She pointed her finger at the teacher, shouting, 'Is that the barsterd?' The boy nodded, and without a second thought the woman reached inside the big shawl that hung around her massive shoulders and pulled out a heavy length of wood, setting about the luckless man with some vigour, encouraged by the shouts and cheers from the boys in the class. It's quite possible that real harm could have been done if the head teacher and a couple of the other masters hadn't appeared in time to pull the woman away. The mother was escorted off the premises, and that was the end of the matter. The school kept quiet, the teacher learnt his lesson, the boy's status in the class was raised and the mother added another victory to her list of battles against authority. All's well that ends well.

IO

Bit of a Lark

During the day there weren't many cases of real violence in the streets. At night it was a different matter: as a gang you didn't venture into the streets of another gang unless you were looking for trouble. Singly or in pairs was quite safe, you were no threat. Mob-handed meant only one thing, and then out came any weapon that might be to hand. Later, as we turned into young men, knuckle-dusters and coshes all became part of our armoury.

During the summer months, when the evenings were long and drawn out, the temptation to liven things up a bit was always present. We had been banned from the playing fields at the Foundling Hospital in Bloomsbury (now called Coram's Fields) because of our 'unruly behaviour' and we wondered where else to go. 'Let's take a stroll down to the Cross.' The trouble with that innocent suggestion was that, to get to the Cross, you had to go over Sidmouth Street, not a good idea if you wanted a peaceful evening. The Sidmouth Street gang would see to that. But it wasn't something that us boys lost any sleep over, to us it was the natural way of life. So long as our boisterous behaviour didn't cause problems with the law, the grown-ups seldom bothered their heads over a few bloodied noses. 'Serve yer right, shouldn't have got in the way of 'is fist' was the typical retort of a father to a son coming home with a damaged conk.

On a Saturday afternoon a trip down to Somers Town or the market in Chapel Street could yield some fruit. None of us had any cash and to get a handful of apples or oranges we had to nick what we wanted while the stallholder had his attention diverted. This was a risky business as stallholders were known to have eyes up their backsides, in the form of the younger men and boys of the family. Nevertheless, undeterred and full of the spirit of adventure, off we went to the market.

Not one of us gave a thought to the idea that we were stealing other people's property. No: to our young minds it was a lark. But in the eyes of the law, property was sacred and the local magistrates had a nasty habit of sending young men of my tender years to 'homes of correction', not a nice experience. There was one lad in our street who had done two years in one of these places. His name was Charlie Stokes and he was older than me, being in the senior boys when I was in the junior. Everyone knew about Charlie and his mum and dad. Charlie had a brother, Freddy, about eight years older, who earned his living as a professional boxer; he was reckoned to be quite handy with his dukes. But Freddy wanted a lifestyle way beyond what he got for bashing other young men around and so spent half his life doing time for breaking and entering. Young Charlie, quite naturally, worshipped his big brother and did his best to follow in Freddy's footsteps. Unfortunately for him his lack of ability in the art of fisticuffs left him with but one other recourse – he started mixing with a gang of lads from Collier Street, which was just off the Pentonville Road, and Charlie ended up before the beak in the court in King's Cross Road. The first time he went down for six months, and the second time saw him put away for eighteen months. In our eyes Charlie was an old lag. Anyway, Charlie came out of the second stretch a completely different person: anything that signalled danger he shied away from; he had been utterly subdued. The cowed way in which Charlie Stokes mooched around was a constant reminder of what lay in store for us if we transgressed.

My brother John and I made regular Saturday morning trips to any one of the giant produce markets of central London. We started these foraging trips when I was seven and John was just into his sixth year. After John went to live with our gran he used to come round to Compton Street on a Saturday morning and Mum could be relied on to put some rashers of streaky bacon in the frying pan, cut up four huge doorsteps of bread and with all that food stuffed down our gullets we sallied forth to the challenge of the market.

We knew that a sack of potatoes and greens could easily be collected off the pavements at the Garden. At Smithfield meat market, what the traders didn't sell by ten in the morning was generally reckoned to be a throwaway job, and it was our intention that any throwing away should be done in our direction: once we even picked up a whole leg of lamb.

There were two drawbacks to a Smithfield trip, the first being that everything collected had to be eaten that day as it went off by the next. The second was the amount of opposition. The youth of the East End gathered en masse at Smithfield on a Saturday morning where there were always fights over possession. No: far better and simpler to be satisfied with the easy pickings at Covent Garden.

The wages that our mum received for her weekly work were too meagre to feed us throughout the week, which meant that without our Saturday supplement the four of us would be down to turnip stew and whatever bits of scrag end meat Mum was able to scrounge from the local butcher who, luckily for us, was a leading member of the local Baptist church of which mother was also a member.

Come Saturday morning, bright and early, having gulped down the bacon sarnies, we were out of the house with our mum shouting her instructions down the stairs: 'Behave yerselves and don't get run over crossing Kingsway and bring back some firewood and pot 'erbs.' By the time the instructions concerning the 'pot 'erbs' reached us we were well on the way to Russell Square.

The rest of the route took us by way of Museum Street, Drury Lane, Long Acre and finally into the mountains of debris that marked the site of the biggest fruit and veg market in the country. All around there were piles of damaged fruit and all manner of different vegetables waiting to be collected up and stashed into the largest wooden box we could find. In less than half an hour we could fill the box to the brim. But our enthusiasm for quantity could prove to be too much.

The overflowing box became too heavy to pull along without breaking the string. So there we would be, two scruffy kids, sitting in the gutter trying to decide what to dump and what we could drag home. At least there was no shortage of string.

And so homewards, back out of Long Acre, through Great Queen Street and along to Southampton Row where stood one of our favourite stopovers: the Holborn Cake and Biscuit Shop. If the cake shop was empty we could have a go at getting some stale cakes for free. We played on our scruffy appearance, dirty and dishevelled, our socks around our ankles, grubby arms outstretched: 'Got any stale cakes, missus?' The lady who ran it was desperate to keep up appearances and could hardly be blamed for wanting to see the back of this pair of street Arabs as quickly as possible. In no time at all a bag of old cakes and biscuits changed hands and we were on our way, scoffing down stale and broken examples of the pastry cook's art that our mum could never afford to buy.

Eventually, we'd get our loot back to our waiting mum who, after evaluating the spoils, began sorting out the little extras she always gave to the old lady who lived in the rooms below us. That night it was off to bed with a good vegetable stew in our bellies.

Whether it was the Garden, Smithfield or Billingsgate, the routine hardly ever varied except, of course, that only Covent Garden supplied the route through Cream Cake Land.

11

The Bear

It was on the streets that we found our amusement and the variety was endless. Nearby we had the three main line railway stations: King's Cross, the home of the London and North Eastern Railway Company, Euston Station, in Euston Road, and the far better St Pancras, which together housed the London, Midland and Scottish Railway. Those three stations acted like a magnet to us boys.

First there were the steam engines themselves: huge monsters belching smoke and steam as they pulled into the station, along with the clanging of metal and the shouts of the porters, the whole station pulsating with the hustle and bustle.

Quite often, when we were at a loss for something to do, one of the boys might suggest a trip down the station, St Pancras being the favourite since it was the easiest station to bunk out of if we got chased by the guards. There, if we were lucky, we would get to carry a passenger's luggage to the nearest hotel. This didn't happen often as any attempt to do the station porters out of earning a bob or two would get us a cuff round the ear. And then there were the railway police who would lose no opportunity to chase us out of the station.

Behind both St Pancras and King's Cross was 'the coal base', the area where mountains of coal were stacked to supply the insatiable hunger of the steam engines. The coal that the steam engines used was not the usual small nuggets that the coalman brought around in his hundredweight sacks. The stuff in the coal base came in super-large lumps, so big that it was only possible to get four into a sack. This was our main source of free fuel.

A raid down the coal base had to be planned. A couple of boys were sent ahead to determine the strength of the railway police. Then, as soon as night fell, and having sussed out the opposition, we would bunk over the wall and throw huge lumps of coal over to our waiting mates. The drawback was that, if you were caught, it meant an appearance in the local police court charged with theft, and this spelled real trouble as it meant that our parents had to pay up. So the winter had to be really cold for us to raid the coal base.

Further behind the stations were the stables. This was another place to earn a little cash. 'Clean yer 'orse darn, mister?' Sometimes we really struck lucky and were offered as much as sixpence to perform this task which meant not only washing and brushing down the horse, or horses, but also cleaning out the stables.

These horses were enormous beasts, and to satisfy their thirst there were horse troughs situated along the main thoroughfares. The horses pulled in to drink and at the same time got rid of the water they had drunk at the last stop. The gallons of urine cascading along the kerbside on its way to the nearest drain hole didn't seem to bother anyone.

Once, on one of our forays to the coal base in which our whole gang was involved, we accidently alerted the railway police and got chased out. One of the boys dropped his school cap, which unfortunately had his name inside. None of us gave this any thought. We had got away, and once back in our street we shared out the spoils, one huge lump each.

A couple of days go by and I'm indoors for a change helping my mum with her housework. The bell clangs away and the next thing we see is the Bear standing outside on the landing. In that confined space he really looked like a bear, he was enormous.

We all knew his name and my mum greeted him: 'Hello, Mr Thomas, what brings you here?' 'Good evening, Mrs Gregg, I'd like a word with young Victor, if you don't mind.' Mum gave me a look. 'Now what games 'ave you bin up to, Victor?' The Bear quickly put my mum at ease. 'Nothing to worry about, missus.' And then he pulled up our one remaining chair and looked me in the eye. 'Now, young man, tell me when you was last round the coal base.' By this time my mum was getting a bit hot and bothered. 'Now, Victor, you tell Mr Thomas the truth.' I could almost feel my mother beginning to cry. The Bear must have sensed this, too. 'Now, now, Emily don't you fret, I'm not here to nick 'im, just give him a friendly warning.' The Bear carried on: 'When I came up the stairs the first thing I set me eyes on is them big lumps of coal that you didn't break up after you and your mates pinched them from the base a couple of nights ago. Why did you pinch them? You know that thieving can get you and that lot you hang around with into real trouble?' 'I wanted to keep my mum warm, she ain't got the money to keep buying coal.' Silence for a few seconds. 'What about a nice cup of tea, Emily?' said the Bear, but Mum was still calling him Mr Thomas. My mum made the tea while the Bear gave me a lecture on how 'ard it was for my mum bringing up her children all on her own without a man to help. There was nothing untoward about the use of mother's Christian name, since everybody knew that the Bear knew everyone's business and nobody expected him to worry about formalities. All the same, I sensed that he was more than a little interested in my mum who, despite the toil and stress, was still a very attractive woman, especially to a man who had lost his wife less than six years before.

The Bear finished his cuppa and with a look at me said, 'You tell your mates to keep away from the coal base, young man. Always think of yer mum and don't cause me any more bovver.' And with that little homily the Bear left. 'Good job for you lot that Mr Thomas is such a good man,' says my mum. 'Not all policemen are as good as 'im.'

The greatest fun of all came from our forays up the other end into the West End. There us kids spent our time doing our best to annoy the toffs, that's of course if they ignored our pleas of 'Gisusasprazeemister' (spare us a tanner, mister).

Another ploy was to stand outside one of the big hotels, where the doorman reigned in all his splendour: black coat and tails, shiny top hat, spotless white gloves and campaign medals polished until they dazzled the eyes. This individual imperiously summoned taxis for the departing guests and beckoned to his underlings to carry the luggage of the incoming clientele, while pocketing an endless flow of tips and largesse which all guests seemed obliged, by custom, to hand over. It was here that we started operations.

Taking care to stand well back so as to dodge the occasional swipe, we gathered by the railings outside the main door. 'Wotcher get all those medals for, mister?' 'What you do in the war, mister?' ''Ere, mister, is yer name Fatty Arbuckle?' 'Come on, mister, givusasprazee.' Back would come the reply, 'Bugger off, yer little turds, or I'll get the rozzers.' The mention of the rozzers was an outright declaration of war. To show what we thought of him and his posh hotel a couple of us undid our trousers and started weeing in the gutter. This act of outright defiance always worked and without fail the doorman, sensing that all was lost, gave in by slinging a couple of sixpenny pieces along the pavement. 'I'll get the lot of yer one of these fine days, yer little whippersnappers.' On one occasion there were four of us out one afternoon; it must have been in the school holidays. One of us was a lad whose hair was a brilliant red. We used to call him 'Bloodnut'. After trying without success to cadge some money from the doorkeeper at the Frascatti restaurant at the start of Oxford Street, we are now outside Waring & Gillow, probably the biggest and poshest furniture shop in the whole of London. It stood on the corner of Oxford Street and Upper Regent Street by Oxford Circus. The huge mahogany front doors swung between two highly polished marble pillars and were guarded by a doorkeeper whose job it was to open the doors of the taxis and private cars as they drew up, salute the customers with a flourish and open up the great front doors with a mighty swing of his arms and shoulders.

What attracted us to this individual was his uniform. Although, like others of his breed, he had a chestful of medals, all highly polished, his coat had no brass buttons; everything was either green or black, even the leather strap that went over his shoulders and was attached to the wide belt round his waist. He wasn't the usual bulky type that we were used to taking the mickey out of. The four of us stood along the kerbside eyeing this bloke up, each of us thinking how best to get him to hand over the dibs.

'Now you lads, 'oppit.' 'Oi, guv'nor, why ain't yer got a red coat like all the others?' 'Was yer in the Salvation Army?' 'Oi, mister, was you in the war?' This barrage of questions was fired out at the top of our voices. We were trying it on, but this man didn't react like all the others; he just ignored us as if we weren't there. It began to cross our minds that we were on a loser. Then a big car drew up and Greenie opens the door. 'Good afternoon, General,' says the doorkeeper. 'Afternoon, Johnson,' says this man, who is now helping his wife out of the car. 'I see you've got some admirers.' ''Fraid so, General, they're trying their arm, goes with the job sort of.' The man who the doorman calls 'General' gives us a look. 'Go back through the years, Johnson, do you recognise them?' ''Fraid so, General.'

The general put his hand into his pocket and brought out a coin. He looked at his wife, she nodded, he pointed to our mate Bloodnut, and said, 'Share this between yourselves and let this gentleman get on with his job.' Then he passed over a shilling piece and the pair of them swept through the doors that 'Johnson' was holding open for them. 'Why did he do that, mister?' 'Because 'e's a good man. Now lose yerselves.' And then he too disappeared inside the store.

Having some dosh in our pockets we decided to retrace our steps back to another cake shop we knew, Cossevelors by name, and get some stale cakes and a bottle of R White's Lemonade. We were rich.

Another source of entertainment was bunking into the London Zoo in Regent's Park. The entertainment came from the keepers who, being able to tell at a glance that we didn't have two halfpennies for a penny, let alone the sixpence entry fee, chased us all around the Zoo.

Regent's Park had quite a large lake. This lake was a rendezvous point for fishing expeditions. The mums manufactured nets out of old stockings, fixed them with a piece of wire to a bamboo cane, and, so armed, carrying sandwiches and some of us with a penny to spend, off we'd set to spend the day fishing for tiddlers. 'And don't come back here soaking wet.'

The day ended when it was impossible to cram another tiddler into the jam jars. Naturally, when we finally arrived back home to proudly display our catch, the poor fish were lifeless, as dead as doornails.

In the summer, a favourite source of enjoyment was the walk to the Tower of London. At low tide it was possible to swim in the river. This was an extremely dangerous pastime and being swept out by the tide was always on the cards. Sometimes the word went around that some boy had drowned. This untimely fate never befell anyone I knew, although I did once have to rescue my brother John from a watery grave when he slipped into the Thames while we were larking about on the steps of Cleopatra's Needle. We both got a walloping on that occasion for coming home soaking wet.

There were three cinemas in the area: the Euston Cinema, which stood near the corner of Judd Street and the Euston Road, the Tolma, up the other end of the Euston Road in Tolma Square, and the Cobo, so named because it was situated in Copenhagen Street, a little way up the Caledonian Road (the Cally). All three of them were right down to earth flea pits or bug huts. When we could afford the price of entry, threepence (or twopence in the case of the Cobo), off we went to witness the exploits of the famed Tom Mix, Bronco Bill and other favourites.

There were times when not all of us could come up with the money for the tickets. Those who could pay went in and took up seats near the exits, even if it meant threatening the kids who were already sitting there. The attendant who always stood by the doors was told that one of our lot had fainted; the other kids, realising that a 'bunk in' was being set up, made it their business to keep the attendant busy while one of us opened the door and let our mates in. Then we sat on the wooden benches and cheered our heroes as they chased the Indians halfway across America, huge shouts and much stamping of feet as another redskin bit the dust.

Although these were, of course, all silent films there was nothing silent about the audience: loud boos if the baddies seemed to be getting the upper hand, the boos soon turning to cheers as the villains got their come-uppance.

When Mother learnt about our session at the bug hut (always on Saturdays), she spread a large piece of newspaper on the table, out came the fine-tooth comb, and there our scalps were searched for signs of fleas and other vermin.

Then there was the Tonbridge Club, named after the sponsor, a large public school situated in Tonbridge, Kent, which must have raised quite a large amount of money to get the project going. A completely new building on the corner of Cromer Street and Judd Street had been erected to accommodate this philanthropic venture. The senior boys at the school had a roster in which they took it in turns to come up to London to supervise the activities: classes in dancing for the girls, cricket, football and boxing for the boys.

In vain they tried to teach us the rules of cricket and football. Their failure was complete when it came to what they termed 'fair play'. The local youth had their own ideas as to what was fair and what wasn't. Their sports master sometimes put in an appearance. Boxing was his speciality, and we had a proper ring, complete with proper boxing gloves. This well-meaning individual attempted to teach us the rudiments of the Queensberry rules, but unfortunately for him the contestants came from streets where there was only one rule – give no quarter.

In the summer we went as far as the Round Pond in Kensington Gardens to watch the posh people sailing their model boats. What a sight my brother and I must have presented, a couple of scruffy kids in our short trousers (well patched) with our socks hanging round our ankles. If Mother had earned a good bonus she sometimes gave us sixpence each, enough to get a return ticket to Edgware on the Northern Line of the underground from King's Cross. The ticket cost us fourpence each return. If by chance we lost our return tickets, which we often did, a pair of doleful eyes would get us past the ticket inspectors.

The most exciting part of the journey was when the train emerged from the tunnel and burst into open countryside. Once out of the station it was a short walk to a land of country lanes and open fields filled with sheep and cows.

On one trip we were approached by a man who asked us if we were lost and where we came from. 'We come up on the train from King's Cross.' 'Where's that then?' said the man. I didn't know where King's Cross was except that the train went there and that's where we lived with our mum. John moved behind me, making sure that I was between him and the man who, dressed in his farmyard clothes, looked a fearsome character. It ended up with the man showing us all over his sheds where he kept his hens and pigs. The pigs really frightened brother John: 'I don't like the smell, let's go home.' For me things were just getting interesting, especially when the woman of the house appeared with a jug of lemonade and some slices of bread and jam and a couple of bits of fruit cake. It was the first time I had ever seen cake that appeared to have more fruit in it than cake. On the way back to the station John slipped into a muddy pond we had discovered in a field that we thought might be a shortcut. He was soaking wet all the way home. I think he got a whack from our gran. I made myself scarce.

Everything was an adventure; even looking into the shop windows of the West End transported us into another world, a world, funnily enough, against which we held no grudge. We were poor, they were rich, that was the way it was. Looking back I suppose that if I was asked 'What's being rich?' my answer would have been: 'Don't know, mister.'

12

Picking Up Tips

Four o'clock and the bell has clanged its message that the day's schooling has finished. As one, the entire class surges towards the door and freedom. Mr Jones, our arithmetic teacher, picks up his cane as if to attempt to impart some element of restraint but then sits down again, probably thinking to himself, 'Well, that's another day over.' The little gang of four of which I am a member is discussing ways to fill in the time before going home. ''Oo's got any money?' Teddy Baldock, who is nearly ten and the acknowledged leader of our small group, asks the question. It turns out that we are all broke. Meanwhile, Tommy, the smallest and youngest of us, has attracted the attention of Mr Reid the gardener because he's been throwing stones at Mr Reid's pride and joy, the flower-beds. Mr Reid charges towards us with his favourite weapon, the huge broom with the spiky bristles. We all do a bunk, sticking our tongues out at him: 'Carn't catch us, baldy.' Now we're out of the gardens and in the street, where there's a copper standing on the corner. He looks to be too big for us to take the mickey out of, but Teddy gives him a bit of lip. 'Wot yer looking at, fatty?' and off we run again. We all desperately need to buy some sweets, Teddy wants some of the new chewing gum like the film stars use, I'd be content with a pennyworth of hundreds and thousands because they last longer. In the end it's decided that a trip to the station might result in a turn for the better as regards our lack of cash. If we can get to carry someone's luggage to a waiting taxi or bus we might get as much as sixpence, so off we troop, singing and cat-calling, off up the slope and into St Pancras Station.

Within five minutes we've been chased out by the railway police. Change of plan. We lie doggo outside the huge entrance arch and soon our patience is rewarded: a man and a woman leave the station and the man is struggling to carry a big case and a couple of little ones. The woman has a case as well but her load is a bit lighter. 'Where yer want to get to, mister?' I ask the man and respectfully touch my cap with the back of my hand, a trick I have copied from watching the doormen at the big hotels. I have noticed that when they salute the customers they always get a tip. 'We have to get to Camden Town, son. Is there a bus?' 'No bus, mister, yer got to get a number seventeen tram. We'll carry yer bags to the tram, 'taint far.' So the man hands over the smallest of the bags and we set off to St Pancras Way, which is just round the corner except that we take him the long way round, hoping he might hand over something extra. We're expecting a sixpence at the least. We dump him at the tram stop and wait until the seventeen comes into view. 'There's yer tram, mister', and we hold out our grubby little hands, he gives us two sixpences and the woman bends down and gives Tommy a big kiss.

13

Tar Blocks and Cricket

We didn't have playing fields or anything like that, but it was a simple matter to put a couple of articles of clothing in the middle of the road to act as goalposts, and, with a ball made out of rolled-up newspaper tied together with string, that would be it. There were no cars cluttering up the streets. Sometimes a game was arranged with the kids in an adjoining street. Naturally the only rule in the book was to get the ball between the opposing goalposts by any means possible. This could be done by kicking, punching, shoving and pushing. The one thing that was considered completely out of order was kicking somebody when they were on the ground. Always on the lookout for more exciting action than a mere game of footer, the shout of 'Foul' gave us the excuse to end the game and start a bundle. Generally the bundle would go on until one side got the worst of it and called it a day, or the police appeared, in which case both sides hurriedly called a truce followed by a smart disappearing act, or, in the terminology of the day, 'we did a scarper'.

Footer was one thing, cricket on the other hand was far more dangerous, at least for the local residents. A wicket chalked up on a lamp post or perhaps on a suitable brick wall marked out the scene of action. A bat was usually made out of a piece of wood and the ball was probably one of the solid rubber balls that were popular at the time. Once the game started it went on until, sooner or later – generally sooner – the ball ended up going through somebody's window. Cricket in the streets was discouraged by the adults who, after all, were our own parents.

Another job we did, mainly in the winter months, was to collect tar blocks. In those days most roads were either paved with wooden or granite blocks. The word going around that a certain road or street was about to be resurfaced was the only signal needed for us to gather with our sacks and wait our chance to raid the stacks of old blocks and bring home as many as possible. They were much cheaper than coal, but, after a week's burning, the chimney became completely blocked by glutinous, foul-smelling tar, causing the rooms to fill up with smoke and fumes. The local chimney sweeps earned a bomb thanks to those blocks.

14

Hop-picking in Kent

J ust after I went into the senior boys' school Mother announced that we were going to have a holiday in the country. We were going 'hop-picking'. Emmy was to stay with our gran as she was considered too young for the rigours of this method whereby the Kent hop farmers got their harvest picked on the cheap. The trip was organised by the local Baptist church. The farmer involved was a dignitary of the Baptist community in that part of Kent. Although the annual migration to the hop fields was a regular feature in the lives of the boys around me, this was a completely new experience for Mother and us two kids.

Mum was given a piece of paper which explained the whole programme, from leaving our house to coming home the following week. It seems that the farmer had come to an agreement with the church that, instead of the hop-pickers signing on for the whole harvest, about four to five weeks, the church guaranteed that any families that returned home would be replaced by new arrivals. The farmer was on to a good thing because he didn't have to worry that the 'out of towners', as we Londoners were called, would follow the lead of the more experienced pickers who were known to down tools after the second or third week and demand another sixpence a bin or a bushel. I don't think Mum earned any extra money for the week we toiled in the hop fields; it was just a way of getting out of the filth of London – which we exchanged for the filth of the hop fields. The day before we were due to leave it was all excitement. Mother borrowed a pram, one with four big wheels, and we filled it up with all the gear that Mum had been told was needed for the coming week, mostly spare clothing, but nothing 'posh' (as if we had anything that could have been remotely called 'posh'). The charity provided us with a pair of wellington boots each, telling us that if they didn't fit we could change them when we reached the farm. All we had to do was get to London Bridge Station by ten in the morning.

Mum got us out of our beds at the crack of dawn and by seven we were on our way. John and I knew full well that the walk never took more than an hour, but mother was adamant: 'Best to be on the safe side.' We trudged our way to the station, Mum pushing the pram, John and I running ahead, looking into the shop windows and revelling in the novelty of the occasion. Our small, happy threesome arrived at the station a good two hours early, but even so there were quite a number of the group already there.

At nine the church dignitaries arrived, our names were taken and, with instructions to keep away from the edge of the platform, the great adventure started. This was the first time we had travelled outside the area we called 'home'. What excitement: we were going on a real steam train. 'Are we going to the seaside, Mum?' 'Shut the window, Victor, we'll all be covered in soot.'

Mother told us what we had to do. 'You can play around in the evening, but during the daytime we all work with everyone else at the picking. Don't be rude to anyone and show respect to the farmer and his family. If it wasn't for them and the church we wouldn't be having any holiday.' (The farmer turned out to be like the rest of his breed: get the crop in by any and all means. You could hardly blame him – the hop harvest lasted about five weeks and if the crop got musty or too wet the farmer's year of hard labour went down the drain.)

The train pulled into a station right out in the country. Then we had to wait for another train. This one only had three coaches which were very old, not like the ones that we were used to seeing at King's Cross or St Pancras. In we all piled and the train chugged along a branch line and finally pulled up with a hissing of steam and rattling of chains. There was not a house in sight and Mum had to push the pram along a path, through a couple of fields, through bridle lanes where the trailing brambles tore at our faces and hands and, of course, our legs; boys never wore long trousers in those days. Finally, we arrived at some sheds. Some were joined together, some built in twos with wooden walls and corru-gated-iron roofs. These were our halls of residence, one family to a shed. We were lucky there was only three of us: some of these families would have the mum and dad and as many as four children. Some had brought their cats and dogs and one couple even had a caged bird. Finally, everyone was sorted and then the man we were told was the overseer sat us down in an adjoining barn-like structure which had a roof but no walls. We were told that this was the dining room and, sure enough, a trolley was wheeled in with some hot stew, platefuls of home-baked bread followed by large containers full of sweet tea; this was more like it.

I had the feeling that our mum was a bit shocked when, after our meal, the overseer introduced us to the facilities. We were shown the toilets, a long shed with a wooden plank with holes in it. When you had answered the call of nature you were expected to fill a large jug with water from an outside tap, sluice it down the hole and then cover the hole with a wood-framed piece of canvas.

The wash-houses were of similar construction, one for men and one for women, and, of course, no hot water. By the time we reassembled back at the huts a huge farm cart had arrived and some farmhands were unloading bits of furniture: a wooden-slatted cot for each member of the family and a table. The cots were made so that they could be placed one on top of the other to save space. John being the youngest was assigned the bottom bunk, I was on the top and Mum's bed was against the opposite wall. The room was divided by a curtain that hung from a wire strung along the length of the room. The only other object was a pot-bellied wood-burning stove. I never measured the room but, thinking back, I guess it was about twelve feet across and perhaps fourteen feet wide. Next arrived some palliasses which we stuffed with straw – these were our mattress and pillows. There was no means of illumination. Afterwards we learnt that the regulars brought their own paraffin lamps.

As the evening approached, we became aware of a strange overpowering odour: the pungent smell of the hops.

We were woken when it got light by one of the farm boys going around and blowing a whistle. Mum was up like a shot and opened the door. Outside, visibility was down to about three feet, the whole camp was enveloped in a thick, soft, clinging mist, on top of which it was freezing cold. 'Come on you two, get your lazy bodies out of them beds and go and wash.' 'It's freezing, Mum.' 'Do the two of you good, put some colour in yer cheeks.' Our mum was relentless. 'Come on, I'm not 'aving the pair of you layabouts showing me up, and I'll be looking be'ind yer ears, I don't want to see any tide marks.' When we returned to the shed she gave us the once over: 'I'll scrub the pair of you tonight, you're not getting away with that cat's lick.'

The only thing I remember about the breakfast was the horrible concoction that went by the name of porridge. It was even worse than I had experienced at the Shaftesbury, and nowhere as good as our mum's. However, the porridge was followed by big trays of fried bacon, eggs and beans and as much bread as we wanted. Everyone helped themselves; not a crumb was left on the trays. Then, hunger satisfied, it was off for our initiation as hop-pickers.

The morning mist had cleared and, with the sun shining, the dew slowly dried off. Down to the lines we trooped. The smell of the hops was by now overpowering. I was sent off to find brother John who had disappeared in the general mêlée. It took me a full hour and when I finally located him he was sitting under a small tree crying his eyes out. He had got himself lost. When I returned him to the arms of my anxious mum, she said, 'Keep your eyes on your brother, Victor, it's the sudden change. John carn't cope like you.'

There were about a dozen of us in our group sitting on stools around a long bench. On top of the bench there was a big long sack. There was a farm worker with a long pole whose job it was to pull the lines of hops off the wires that they grew along and on to the table. As the lines came down to the table some of the branches got entangled with the hair of those women, like Mum, who had not covered their hair with a scarf. On that first day plenty of time was wasted while the women tried to untangle their hair from the vines. Those far-sighted men and women who had managed to escape this predicament were now busy picking the hops off the vine stalks and filling the sacks with hops and making sure that no leaves went in.

At about eleven in the morning a whistle was blown and everyone stopped. Mum propelled me and John to the food shed where a light lunch had been laid out by the farmer. Bread and cheese and a sort of salad. 'Don't show me up by gulping yer food down like pigs.' That was our mum telling us not to be greedy. Everyone helped themselves, no one counted how many slices of bread and cheese you had, and after about twenty minutes we were all back at the bench slaving away at the hops. There was another break in the afternoon and then slog on until the overseer blew his whistle signifying the end of the day's toil. Then we trudged back through the fields to the huts or sheds, where we had a wash before sitting down to whatever dinner was served up. As soon as dinner was finished, Mum gave us our orders: 'Go into the woods and get some firewood.' This was for the pot-bellied stove; everyone was doing the same thing because the only possible way to get rid of this sort of sticky dirt was with lashings of hot water. Our mum's list of what to bring had included the biggest kettle you could get hold of.

Once we'd got the wood, Mum set about boiling the water, and there we were, me and my brother John, stark naked, while Mum set to work on the grime we had accumulated in the course of our first day's work. By the time she finished the long bar of Sunlight soap had shrunk by half: 'And don't get dirty like that any more or it will be a repeat performance tomorrow.' There was no way that John and I wanted a repeat of that torture so we swore to our mum that we would keep ourselves clean in future

By seven in the evening some of the men were already on their way to the village pub while the rest of the group sat around a big campfire. John and me had never experienced anything like it, with the smoke getting in our eyes and the sparks from the huge fire leaping up into the night sky. The women spent the evening gossiping about the day's goings on and then Mum brought out her mandolin and another man fished out an accordion and the evening came alive to the sound of singing. Us boys were very proud of our mum; she was much in demand.

John and I were on our own there as all the kids came

from different areas and we knew none of them. The first item on my agenda was letting all the other kids know that 'anyone taking the piss out of my bruvver is going to cop it'. It wasn't that I felt belligerent towards the other kids; it was what I saw as the proper way to protect John, who I always thought was a bit on the slow side. Anyway, we kept to ourselves and the holiday ran its course without my getting into any trouble.

Then all of a sudden it was time to go. I'm sure our mum enjoyed herself but we never went again. I think the pole in the toilets was too much for her.

15

Mr James and His Canes

I was now eleven and along with all the other eleven-year-olds I was sent to one of the three senior boys' schools in the area. I ended up in the roughest of the lot. The streets surrounding this establishment were completely run-down. The people who lived there could hardly be blamed for giving up hope, and yet there was a never-say-die spirit of survival and it showed in the way people lived. On the one hand they circled the wagons and thumbed their noses at all authority, but come a royal occasion or a national day of celebration out would come the flags and the bunting, all home-made, but bringing the dull streets to life. At school the whole of the new intake was marched into the main hall where the senior teacher laid down the law which we were to abide by. He had a habit of accentuating each sentence by whacking his cane on his desk. 'You boys will turn up each morning clean and tidy.' (Whack.) 'You boys will stand up when a teacher comes into the classroom.' (Whack.) And so on. Throughout this oration his eyes swept along the two lines of boys standing in front of him. As soon as he had finished, another man came in. This was no less than the headmaster himself who turned out to be an entirely different character. The senior teacher was built like Charles Atlas, while the head was short and had a benign smile on his face, indicating that here was a man who wouldn't hurt a fly. The big stick and the velvet glove.

The message was that we were here for the next three years, after which, at the age of fourteen, we would be thrust out into the big nasty world. 'Just get stuck in, boys, and learn what you can, you will not get any second chances.' So said the headmaster. Then he disappeared into his office leaving us to the tender mercies of the muscle man who went on laying down the law.

I didn't know it at the time but I later learnt that this was a school that made other boys tremble at the thought of being sent there. Each teacher had his own classroom, and me and the other boys in my class filed into the room where the most feared of the teachers held court: the dreaded Mr James. Mr James didn't talk like any of the other teachers; this was because he came from Wales and the people there all worked under the ground digging out coal. Those who were too clever for the coal job came to England and became teachers.

Mr James had a selection of canes that he kept hanging on the wall behind his desk. When we were all sitting down he stood up behind his desk and glared down at the tribe he was to teach. After studying us for some moments he carefully selected the stick that he fancied and then, without warning, brought it down with a resounding *thwack* on the top of his desk, sending clouds of chalk dust billowing into the air.

Mr James was the geography teacher and he spent three sessions teaching us about India. 'Right, boys, this morning our subject is India, same as last week. Now, which one of you bright lot is going to tell us the name of the capital of India?' Up went the hands of half the class. 'Delhi, Mr James.' 'Good show,' said the teacher. 'Now, who's bright enough to tell us which side of the continent Karachi is on and which side Calcutta is on?' So effective was this teaching by rote that at least half the class was able to answer. 'You there, yes, you with your mouth full of toffee.' James pointed to one of the young scruffs in the back row who attempted to extract the toffee from his mouth and stick it under the flap of his desk. 'Tell the class, Roberts, why on the map India is coloured in red.' ''Cause it's the British Empire and they all belong to us.' Mr James complimented Roberts on his knowledge. 'And tell us, Roberts, what do we call the people who live in this India that's coloured in red?' Roberts thought about this for a moment. 'Red Indians, sir.' 'Red Indians!' roared James. 'Roberts, are you by any chance trying to be Jack the Lad?' By now the class was roaring with laughter and Mr James could feel his authority slipping away by the second. 'Out here in front, Roberts, bend over.' And poor Roberts, whether his answer about Red Indians was intended as a joke or not, was given a couple of strokes with the cane.

Mr James's methods wouldn't be acceptable today but, good or bad, they worked then. The whacks I suffered were forgotten once the stinging sensation had disappeared. In fact, the boys boasted about their teacher's prowess with the cane, suggesting that they were tougher because they were able to withstand all that he could lay out. And yet all the noise and threats turned out to be a façade behind which the teachers of this supposedly hard-nosed institution gave their all to offer the boys every possible chance to lift themselves out of the gutter.

At Cromer Street School I was introduced to the personal weaponry that replaced the comparatively frail pieces of wood we used at Prospect Terrace. Strips of half-inch brass were heated and bent to a shape that fitted a clenched fist. The finished article was a primitive knuckle-duster, not as heavy as the real thing but hard enough to stop any adversary who cared to chance his luck. Of course, it was no use having this weapon unless the owner had the guts to use it.

A couple of pennies between the fingers of a clenched fist was another widely used method of inflicting damage. With one well-aimed slash the pennies could reduce a face to ribbons. The most important thing was to make certain that whatever tool was carried looked like an article of everyday use. If a lad, even if he was a young boy, was picked up carrying an 'offensive weapon', or the means of 'breaking and entering', it meant a sojourn behind bars, the length of sentence depending on the mood of the magistrate.

In about the second week, during the afternoon break, six or seven of us, all new to the school, were messing about kicking a ball against a wall. Up sauntered a gang of older boys who went straight to the point: 'Oi, you lot, f— off, this is our bit of wall.' This challenge was answered with a blank stare. We all knew that these boys came from Ossulton Street, a particularly tough area by Somers Town, but nobody was going to make the first move of submission. It was now up to the aggressor to prove his point, which he did by giving the biggest of us – me – a right-hander which split my nose open. Blood gushing everywhere and that was it – a bundle. The opposing warriors were finally pulled apart by a couple of the teachers and the whole pack of us were marched up to the headmaster's office.

We all got a right whacking with all sorts of dire threats about further punishment. The head told us that it was us new boys who were the prime culprits, guilty of breaking the peace. 'Whatever you got away with in your last school, it's different here.' I still see the lad who started it all; him and his mates were standing behind the head smirking away. Nobody argued with the head, although, funnily enough, we never got challenged again. Mum gave me another dressing down when she got home that evening: 'You're growing up now, time to think of your future.' If Mum had tried to clip me one I would have let her. We all loved our mums.

All the schools in the area organised outside sports activities. There were about six schools in the King's Cross educational group and every three or four months teams were picked from each school which presented themselves at the allotted playing field, nearly always at Coram's Fields. If a boy was picked to represent the school it was considered a matter of honour.

Our school always won the boxing. If I was lucky enough to win a bout and get one of the little medals I took it home to our mum expecting praise, but Mum never approved of fighting: 'Carn't yer get a medal for something worthwhile?'

I was never able to see Mum's point of view. What I and my mates understood was that if you didn't stand up and fight you were at everybody's mercy, mostly from the boys in the next street. The headmaster, Mr Thornton, played the violin. The geography and history teachers played the cello and the English teacher, Mr Barbour, was a pianist. The other four teachers taught painting, poetry and drawing. The result of this unusual dedication was that the classes were full, and this in a school where the boys were so poor they used to put cardboard in their boots to cover the holes; where socks were a luxury and all the clothes worn by the boys would be hand-me-downs or purchased at the local charity shop, the Crusade of Rescue. If it proved nothing else, it proved that whatever part of society they come from, children are always willing to learn, and the teacher is the crucial element.

Thanks to Mr Thornton we had a school band that used to win prizes and come out ahead of even the local grammar schools. It was Mr Thornton who taught me the rudiments of music and inspired me. 'Keep your bow straight, hold the violin up to your chin, don't let it droop, it's not in need of a lie-down, keep your eye on the music, listen to the beat.' And so on. Mr Thornton never believed in doing things by halves. He just kept us at whatever we were doing until, in his judgement, we were as good as we were ever likely to get.

And so the years continued to pass and we lived happily in Compton Street until my grandparents managed to get accommodation in Kenton Street in the posh Borough of Holborn. And that's where a new stage of my life began.

16

The Move to Bloomsbury

When Mum told me about the move to Gran's house in Kenton Street I wasn't too happy about it. 'But, Mum, I don't know anybody round there. Anyway, it's full of cissy boys, that's wot they are. I've seen 'em, they spend their time talking to girls.' 'If it gets you away from this rough lot round 'ere then that's a good thing. You'll just 'ave to get used to it, and there will be no more bugs and mice and those 'orrible cockroaches and you can join the Boy Scouts when we settle in.' It looked to me as though I was going to suffer a fate worse than death. I didn't view being a Boy Scout with any enthusiasm.

Not all the boys in the neighbourhood viewed the Boy Scouts as a cissy adventure to be avoided at all costs, however. 'Ain't all that bad, in the summer they go camping and the girls go wiv 'em.' 'So what?' 'Well, dontcha know, they all go in the same tent and do it?' 'Do wot?' 'Well, I don't know 'cept they do somefink.' All I knew about women was my mum, my gran and little Emmy, who wasn't so little any more and was the reason that I'd been exiled to the kitchen, but she was still my little sister and if any boy took the mickey out of her I'd be on him like a ton of bricks.

Then one day my Uncle Joe and another uncle, Mum's brother Will, who came from Calthorp Street off the Gray's Inn Road, turned up with a large barrow to transfer our meagre belongings to our new abode. To make matters worse, my mates queued up giving me the hoots. 'Oy, Vic, gonna live with the cissy boys then? We'll come round an' do 'em up if yer want.' At this point my Uncle Sam, who was a big bloke from Kentish Town, threatened them with 'a clip round the ear' that really got them going. I couldn't help feeling proud of my mates; they were frightened of no one.

At last the deed was done and me, Mum, John and little Emmy were settled in on the first floor, still only two rooms, but much cleaner, no gaps in the woodwork for the mice to crawl out of and the windows didn't rattle. The rooms themselves were larger and bigger though the rent was the same.

More than anything it was the front door that made me aware of our sudden change in fortune. For a start the door opened and shut properly; it wasn't hanging on one hinge like the door in Compton Street which was a door in name only. It never closed properly either. Whoever came in last at night used to slide a piece of wood under it to stop it rattling. Some of our neighbours just had an open space, the door having been chopped up for firewood.

This new door had a brass knocker and a big electric push-button bell, all highly polished, as were the three pull knobs for the upstairs bells. Even the door itself had a shine on it. Our new landlord was the Foundling Estate and part of the large Coram Benevolent Institution. And so we were dragged away from the sordid surroundings of our early years. From now on my grandparents took over.

Grandfather was a short, round man with red cheeks and a huge curly moustache. Off he set every morning with his rolling gait on the walk to Hatton Garden where he worked, wearing a black Homburg and swinging his Gladstone bag, a larger than life gold watch chain strung across his ample paunch.

Grandmother was the opposite, tall and angular, her black hair swept up into a tight bun, eyes that looked right through you. She was always dressed in a long black dress which encased her from her ankles to her high, ruffled neckline. She wore a chain around her waist from which dangled various keys, none of which seemed to be used, except the front door key.

This doughty pair lived in the lower part of the house. The kitchen was in the basement in which nearly all our waking hours were spent. Behind the kitchen was the scullery, complete with a huge open boiling pan in which the weekly wash was done (and the Christmas puddings were cooked). The bedroom was at the back on the ground floor, while the front room, or parlour, was reserved for special occasions, like Christmas and birthdays. The centrepiece of the parlour was a large aspidistra, the leaves of which my gran polished religiously once a week.

During the summer months Gran took her place at the window to look out on the street, commenting on the qualities, good and bad, of the neighbours. It was in this front room that brother John had his bed.

This couple deplored the social level that their daughter had sunk to, blaming it all upon my father, 'that scandalous plumber from Kentish Town'. 'You never could trust them as comes from that neighbourhood.' The fact that my grandparents had lost two sons in the Great War while the plumber from Kentish Town had emerged unscathed didn't help matters either.

In those days working people had an almost fanatical allegiance to the royal family. I never went to my mates' homes without seeing the stern eyes of King George and Queen Mary staring down at me from one of the walls. No matter if the rooms were nice and clean, or filthy with flaking plaster and the paper peeling off, the pictures were there for all to see. And, of course, in my grandparents' house, hanging next to the sacred royal photographs, were the pictures of the two sons who had been laid out in Flanders Field. My grandparents were Victorian in their outlook; there was never any messing about. At the meal table you were served according to your station in the household, small boys being last, and not only that, seen and not heard. 'Don't talk with your mouth full!' 'Eat what's given you!' 'Ask permission if you wish to leave the table!' To be certain that discipline was maintained there was a convenient shelf under the edge of the table where resided the CANE, and my grandmother was an expert at wielding that formidable instrument while Grandfather just sat and ate. All the same, they were both good to us. They had realised that Mother was in an impossible situation and had decided to take the weight off her shoulders.

17

The Crusade of Rescue

As soon as we moved into our new home, Grandmother announced that on Saturday we were going to take a walk to the Crusade of Rescue. This emporium had its premises in Tavistock Place, just at the end of Kenton Street. The Crusade was the Oxfam shop of its day, a place with a huge open front, filled to bursting with all sorts of second-hand clothing, all donated by charitable organisations.

So there we were, my brother and I, standing like a couple of goons while Mother and Grandmother debated as to whether some garment or other was appropriate. After the suits came the boots, and once these were selected they were taken to the boot mender who put as many studs into them as possible. By the time we came to wearing them, the soles and heels were almost solid steel. 'And don't let me catch you sliding about on them.'

One afternoon, as I was walking to Grandmother's home, a dog rushed out of a doorway and took a large chunk out of my arm. A passer-by took me home, where Gran doused the gash with iodine and took me to the doctor's to be stitched up. Then off she went to find the owner of the dog. When she found him she set about him with a large shovel she had taken with her for that specific purpose. The poor man ended up in the Royal Free Hospital and Grandmother up before the local magistrate. It turned out that Grandfather, who was a Freemason, was in the same lodge as the beak, so nothing came of it.

The move to Kenton Street also brought us into contact with all the uncles and aunts on the Hamblin side of the family – at least those surviving uncles who had managed to escape the scythe of the Grim Reaper during the war. Uncle Will lived quite near, just off the Gray's Inn Road, but Uncle Tom lived out in the wilds of Epsom. Then there was Uncle Sam and Uncle Joe, who I have already mentioned and who lived in council flats in Rosebery Avenue. All these relatives used to visit us once a month to 'pay the Club', the club being the Sir John Peel Working Men's Mutual Society, of which Grandfather was one of the trustees. Once a month off he toddled to a meeting up in Marylebone Lane, some-times taking me with him.

After handing over the monthly dues he had collected, he would, with much puffing and blowing, assume his place at the committee table alongside the rest of the hierarchy. After the evening farewells came the walk home, often in the company of one or two of the other club dignitaries. A halt was usually made at some drinking establishment. I never saw the inside of these places – 'Just hang about a bit, Victor, small boys not allowed in here' – and while waiting I amused myself thinking about the reception that I knew from experience Granddad was going to get from Grandma.

If by some chance the refreshing nectar had flowed too freely I knew enough to make myself scarce until the almost certain ensuing battle between my gran and her somewhat tipsy husband died down. That said, I never knew my grandfather to get really drunk and incapable; my gran wasn't going to give him the chance.

18

Costermongers in Kenton Street

The move to Kenton Street made life much easier for Mum: for one thing it was simpler for us to keep clean. John was still sleeping downstairs with my grandparents and it seemed to me that they had taken my brother off Mum's hands and adopted him as their own son. As for myself, I used to spend the evenings and nights with my old friends from Wakefield Street. 'What's it like round there, Vic?' 'A load of cissy boys, I reckon' was my verdict.

There were other sights and sounds that were new to us after the move. Being a slightly better off area, it was common for the streets to be targeted by all the various costermongers, especially on a Sunday afternoon. The Muffin Man, walking along in the centre of the road, carried his wares on a large wooden tray balanced on his head, ringing his huge brass bell, 'Muffins, luvly muffins.' Then there was the man who sold shellfish, the Winkle Man. Everyone recognised him, trundling his barrow and announcing his presence with a large motor horn. Then there was the Cat's-Meat Man, the

Fruit and Veg Man, and last but not least, all through the summer months sitting in his old wicker chair and occasionally giving his ice cream a stir, would be Tony the Ice-Cream Man.

There used to be a song the kids would sing, and it went something like this:

> I come all the way from Italia,
> And I find my way down Saffron Hill, how do you feel?
> In winter I sell ches-a-nuts a hotta,
> In summer I sell ice-a-da-cream bigger da top, no taster,
> Hurra, hurra, hurra for the Italian Man.

I almost forgot the organ grinders, nearly all of them ex-service, with one or more limbs missing, reduced to begging as their only means of support. Hard times they may have been, but working people were not slow to throw pennies out of the window, and so music filled the street and the young girls, throwing a rope across the road, ended up skipping merrily away – Salt, Mustard, Vinegar, Pepper, with the rope whizzing around until they all fell to the ground, exhausted.

To my mum's delight I gradually began to mix more with the boys in Kenton Street. Although, if at a loss for something to do I'd go back round to my old mates in Wakefield Street and in no time would be back to the old tricks, one of which was a trip up the Cally to see if we could bunk in to watch the boxing, especially if there was one of our local heroes on the programme.

The boys in Kenton Street weren't interested in boxing, but, as I was to discover, they had other interests, like the swimming pool in Endell Street, which lay on the south side of New Oxford Street. For just twopence you could spend the whole of Saturday morning at the baths. It was in Endell Street that I became aware that there were men who gained much pleasure from associating with small boys and good-looking youths.

It didn't take long to suss out these individuals for what they were really after. I remember there used to be a clique of about four of them, always handing out bags of sweets which, naturally, we accepted: 'Fanks, mister.' Obviously they must have achieved satisfaction with some of the boys but none that I knew. It was through these gentlemen, as we grew older and into our teens, that we were able to get night-time employment in the clubs and cafés of Soho as washers-up.

The work started any time after seven in the evening and then we set to, washing the crockery and cleaning the glasses until ten in the evening. For this we were paid the huge sum of ten shillings a night, which was equal to the amount we were to earn for a week's work when it came time to leave school.

19

Growing Up in Bloomsbury

Bloomsbury, the area we were now living in, was in those days almost a village. People were not born there, they moved there. A person might proudly announce that he 'came from' Bermondsey, or Poplar, or any other place, but you never heard people say that they 'came from' Bloomsbury; more like: 'I am at present in rooms in Bloomsbury.'

Bloomsbury and the area on the other side of the Tottenham Court Road, known as Fitzrovia, was the place in which I was to serve my apprenticeship in the art of growing up. The area was the happy hunting ground of the street girls and the gangs from Soho, just across New Oxford Street, who controlled them.

At the top of the pile was the gang run by the Sabini brothers who had the majority of the girls along with the vice dens and gaming houses. Close on their heels were the equally intimidating Hoxton Mob. These two gangs between them not only owned nearly all of Soho and the West End, but it was a well-known fact that they had Savile Row, the

main police station, well and truly in their pockets. It was the
Hoxton Mob who became one of our main sources of
income, unbeknown to our parents, of course. Mother and
our grandparents strove in vain to keep my brother and me
away from the evils of the area, but if there was money to be
earned then we would offer our talents to earn it. As we
grew out of our short trousers and began to fill out into
young men, the pimps and small-time crooks who had got
used to seeing us around day after day began to buy our
services as watchers or lookouts so they could carry on their
nefarious enterprises in comparative safety.

Mixing with the criminal elements had its dangers. If
you started getting handouts from one of the mobs then
that was the lot you got stuck with, the only trouble being
that at any time you could be attacked by the kids who were
getting dropsy – small retainers – from a rival mob. The six
of us who roamed the backstreets of Soho, Greek Street,
Wardour Street, Frith Street and the like started our life of
'aiding and abetting' by doing the simplest of tasks. The
gangs hung about in the clubs during the daylight hours,
drinking, playing cards and planning their next jobs. They
started by asking us to 'nip darn and get us some fags'. It
wasn't long before we realised that the lot we were doing
these favours for was the infamous Hoxton Mob, cutthroats
and number one villains to a man. 'You boys want to steer
clear of the Sabinis, if they get to know you're hanging
round us, they'd think nothing of slitting yer throat.' Timely
warnings which, because we were earning cash, went in
one ear and out the other.

The Hoxton Mob, as their name implied, originated from Hoxton, in the depths of the East End of London. The Sabinis came from a district much nearer to where our little bunch of tearaways lived, Saffron Hill, an area off the Clerkenwell Road adjacent to Farringdon Road, around the corner so to speak. They were of Italian or, more correctly, Maltese extraction.

All the local ice-cream vendors had to pay their dues to this mob and, of course, all the girls and their pimps had to get permission if they wished to work to the east and north of Cambridge Circus or St Giles Circus. The two gangs didn't encroach on each other's territory and that's how they kept the peace between themselves. It didn't always work and then battles would rage that the police were powerless to stop. Us small, inconspicuous boys were used to keep an eye on the enemy and occasionally, if a job was planned 'up West', it would be let known that a small earner was on for a couple of hours' lookout.

Much later on these two arch enemies had a head-on clash somewhere down in south London. According to what I read it was a right bust-up involving knives, shooters and anything that could do mortal damage. One of the Hoxton boys died of shotgun wounds and a couple of the Sabinis finished up with severe knife wounds. I think this took place in New Cross. What it showed was how far and wide these two gangs spread their tentacles. The final clash between the two gangs was a horrendous battle in 1936, at Lewes race-course, where they were at each other's throats over who was going to control the bookies and the lucrative off-course betting scams.

Our little gang also earned some dropsy from a gang that came from Somers Town, known as the Tolma Gang, presumably named after Tolma Square which was just around the corner. This small mob specialised in breaking and entering. They got all their information from the society columns in the quality papers. They'd read when Lord and Lady Whatsit were out of town or visiting somewhere abroad, then they would spend a couple of days sussing the house out, which was usually in some expensive part of the city, Belgravia, Knightsbridge or the like.

The first bloke in would be the screws man. He gained entry by shinning up a drainpipe. Once on a balcony out came a small putty knife to cut away the putty from a windowpane. Next a small pair of pliers to draw out the tacks that held the glass in. Then, with the help of a sink plunger, the pane was noiselessly removed. Then into the house, down the stairs, open the front door and that would be the screws man's job finished. He departed the scene leaving a couple of men to go over the house while the most important member of the team set about cracking the safe. While all this was going on, us boys scoured the streets in the vicinity on the lookout for the law. As I said, a nice little earner. I never heard that the Tolma Gang ever got nobbled by the law. I finally came to my youthful senses when one of my mates mentioned to some of the elders of the Hoxton Mob that his dad worked as a lighterman on a Thames barge. The gang had been planning a heist on one of the many bonded warehouses that lined the river from Blackfriars all the way down to Wapping Creek. To have a contact who had access to one of the barges would have been like owning a gold-mine.

We boys knew the risks we were running. We all knew that doing a stint in a Borstal was not a pleasant experience: about half a dozen of the older boys had been inside one and what they told us about those establishments was enough to make anyone's hair curl. So we all decided to give Soho and the Hoxton Mob and all the other gangs the drop kick. There were other ways to earn money.

20

Choirboy and Scout

When I was about twelve John and I were dragged round to the church in Woburn Square. The word had gone out that they were short of choirboys: 'Put the two of you on the straight and narrow,' said Grandfather. As an aside he mentioned the news that we would be eligible for the 'Sunday School Outing', soon to take place.

Unfortunately, I had acquired a certain reputation in the area. 'Bit of a scruff, that one.' The vicar was not at all keen. He said he could only take one of us, but what he really needed was a boy who could sight-read a score. He shoved one under my nose, and without hesitation I gave a true rendering of the music. This must have shaken him to the foundations and from that moment on I was flavour of the month. Not that I was in any way keen on the idea of being a cissy choirboy, but to please Mother and my grandparents I stuck with it for nearly nine months. After that, enough was enough.

Although I was hopeless at singing, I used to help the organist out with the musical arrangements. When he found out I was leaving, he promised me the earth to stay on. 'Be a good lad and think of your future.' He even made contact with the headmaster at Cromer Street School. I got a lecture from him as well. I suppose they were both trying their best to help me; after all, it was obvious to them that I did have some talent. For me music was just something I enjoyed but that was all.

Soon after I was press-ganged into the Woburn Square church choir the news went around that there was some Yank who had a big posh car and was going to start up a new Scout Group in Herbrand Street. The vicar expected all of us to turn up at the first meeting; he said it would be like a big party and there would be cakes and ice cream and jellies, followed by games with prizes.

The man responsible for all this had formed a group called 'the Holborn Rovers' and these lads were going around putting cards in all the local shop windows, and the whole area was abuzz with the news. The locals considered the enterprise a good thing: 'About time something was done, keep the little scruffs off the streets.' Or some such words.

The first event was mightily oversubscribed. There was to be a meeting every week and, once they had been accepted, boys were expected to turn up with their uniforms clean and pressed. For any boy whose parents couldn't afford the uniform it would be issued free of charge. The local mums loved it and they loved the man who was organising it all. He was called Ralph Reader and, as well as having an American accent, he was very handsome. He moved and talked like a film star. To top it all, the posh car he owned was an enormous American open-top touring Chrysler which he parked outside the hall where we met. Even though he had all the women swooning and starry-eyed, he used to spend a lot of his spare time in the company of his friend, a gentleman who lived in a block of flats on the edge of Russell Square.

The uniform we had to buy consisted of a pair of blue short trousers, a khaki shirt, a red scarf with grey trimming around the edge and a length of coloured string with a whistle on the end. There was also a belt which, when we could afford to buy one, was meant to carry a vicious looking sheath knife. Finally, there was the hat, wide-brimmed with a pointed top. You could also earn badges by passing various tests and these were sewn on to your shirt.

Ralph Reader himself was actually born in Somerset. He had emigrated to America and become a successful choreographer and stage producer but had for some unknown reason returned to the land of his birth and became a personality in the theatre scene. One evening he was chatting to a small group of us and told us that he had never realised how bad it was for us London kids. He said it was bad in New York but just as grim over here. Reader was sincere in what he was attempting to do. 'The Skipper', as he wanted us to call him, stuck to his task, finally producing his famous *Gang Show* at the Scala Theatre. The event became a centrepiece of the world Scout Movement – and it all started at the 10th Holborn Scout Group.

As my gran had forked out the cash for the uniform I was morally bound to turn up for the weekly parades. Afterwards

I would make my way to my mates in Wakefield Street who scoffed at the whole idea. 'Load of cissy boys, that's what they are, let's go round and bash 'em up.' They never did, but I have to admit I felt the same way. I thought that, somehow, the boys were being used, but I couldn't put my finger on how. I knew where I was with the lads in Wakefield, Sidmouth and Cromer Streets: there was no double talk, a spade was a spade, nothing hidden. I was happy with that and after a while I left the Holborn Rovers; some of them even started calling each other 'Dear' – not my cup of tea at all!

Once I was free from the responsibility of being a well-behaved choirboy, I was soon back with my old Wakefield Street mates. While I had been away a couple of Irish families had moved into the street.

For all the time that I had known them, the leader of the gang was a hard nut by the name of Tommy Spires. Tommy and I had it out together a couple of times over the leadership of the gang and on both occasions I came off second best. But we respected each other and the rest of the gang understood the score. Tommy was top dog and that was that.

Unfortunately for Tommy, around the time that I arrived back in the fold a couple of the new arrivals, Irish boys, began to challenge his authority. 'Well, if you carn't sort 'im out, Tommy, what you expect me to do?' 'Well, I was finkin' that we could sort the two of 'em out together, run 'em off the turf, give 'em a good bashing.' The thought that they might be about to witness a real good bundle was irresistible to the rest of the gang. 'Let's go and sort 'em out then.' When I finally got home that evening I had two split lips and my eye was cut above the lid. I was put through the mangle by my mum and gran: 'Ain't you ever going to grow up? I thought you was told to keep clear of that lot in Wakefield Street.' With my sore head I wasn't feeling in the best of spirits but the two Irish lads were stopped, never to challenge again. Tommy and me were now the best of mates and the gang carried on stronger than ever. Our little leadership struggle had been noted by no less a man than the Bear himself. The lads who had caused all the trouble didn't go to Cromer Street School; they went to the Roman Catholic school a few streets away. In our school the word went around that Tommy and me had seen them off and we stalked around the playground like a couple of gods. That is until we were called in to see the headmaster.

We went prepared for the worst, but, instead of the dreaded cane, Mr Thornton told us to sit down and to listen carefully to what he was about to say. It went something like this. 'I suppose you two consider yourselves unbeatable? The pair of you strutting around like a couple of champion fighting cocks. You're both nearly thirteen years old and in a year's time you'll leave school and be out on the streets trying to earn a living. If you carry on the way you are now you will both spend most of your lives behind bars. As for you, Victor Gregg, I really thought you had something better in you. And you, young Tommy, what do you want out of life, just one fight after another? Is that all you're good for? I think you can do better for yourselves. I want you both off the streets and into the grammar school. It's the only chance you'll have so get stuck in and make something of yourselves.'

With that he dismissed us. We learnt later that our Mr Thornton and the Bear had talked about us and, much to the Bear's satisfaction, Mr Thornton had decided to lay down the law to us.

The amazing outcome was that, almost overnight, Tommy Spires left the gang and ended up at the grammar school in Great College Street. As for me, I knew that I could do better, but I was torn between that and wanting to be with the lads in Wakefield Street.

Part Two

21

Brooklands Boy

My years at Cromer Street School ended when I turned fourteen, at which point I presented myself to the local labour exchange in Penton Street, at the top of Penton-ville Road.

The next week, straight out of school and now in a good pair of second-hand long trousers, I started working for an optical firm just off Rosebery Avenue, on the second floor of an industrial building at the corner of Exmouth Street Market. The firm was called F. G. Optical Company, the F. G. standing for Fritz Gua. The company was a specialist manufacturer of spectacle frames and nearly all the work was carried out by scruffy boys just out of school. Boys like me in other words. Fritz's partner was a Welshman by the name of Lewis, who handled relations with the small workforce. The work was just a means of making a wage in order to have money in your pocket. We earned ten shillings a week, stand-ard for a youngster at the time, half of which I gave to my mum; the remaining five shillings was all mine to spend on clothes, mostly second-hand, and anything else that took my fancy. Paid on Friday and skint by Sunday night, if not before, that was the norm.

I was given the job of operating one of the milling machines that turned out the frames. Oblong pieces of thick plastic were piled up on the bench in the morning. The boys employed in milling had to put a piece of this plastic into a jig and then we milled it out on a cutting wheel which whizzed around at thousands of revs per minute, just a bare cutter protruding from a hole in the bench with no protection of any kind. There was a constant depletion of the workforce due to the regular cutting off of fingers. The Royal Free Hospital in Gray's Inn Road knew the firm well. The factory inspectors used to turn a blind eye and I often wondered if they were being bribed to stay away.

Work started at eight o'clock, with a ten-minute break at ten thirty, then half an hour for dinner for which the firm provided the tea. We ate whatever our mums had provided in the way of sandwiches. Then the final slog until the whistle blew at five thirty. When a mishap occurred such as a finger being cut off, the cry would go out: 'BLOOD UP'. Then, while the victim was whisked away to hospital, one of us was detailed to wash the blood off the wall, and cover it with liberal amounts of distemper to hide the stain. The only employees who were over sixteen or seventeen were the man who cut out the blocks of plastic on a huge bandsaw and the girls who worked in the polishing shop. There were also some men – we were told they were Germans – who worked in a separate room fixing the side pieces to the frames. By the time the boys were old enough to ask for more money they were sacked and a fresh bunch of recruits taken on.

It was during a slack period that Mr Lewis asked me to take a bucket and some polishing kit and go down to the local garage to wash his car, a big American Buick. The garage was the home of the Mount Pleasant Taxi Company. It was run by the son of old man Levy (a well-known character on the London cab scene) who owned Levy's of King's Cross, the parent company, and it was the major taxi firm of the day. This was quite exciting. I used to polish the Buick and then polish it again. Unbeknown to the boss I learnt to drive it around the garage to the amusement of the fitters and cleaners who worked there.

One fine day old man Levy's son came up and asked me if I could 'find the time to wash down a couple of his cars'. 'Not 'arf,' says I, thinking, of course, of the extra money. Tom Levy had a couple of MGs with which he competed at Brooklands, in Surrey, and sometimes Donington, in the Midlands, and it was these cars that he wanted me to keep 'nice and shiny'.

I gave my first job the boot. I had been at it for just eight weeks. My new job as a taxi cleaner at Levy's of Mount Pleasant paid an extra five shillings a week with much better conditions and without the threat of losing my fingers. It was when Tom Levy started taking me to Brooklands that life began to get interesting. It was there that I met all the famous racing drivers of the day, men like Freddie Dixon who used to drive for Riley, Tom Birkett, another character, and last but not least Earl Howe, whose most famous car was a huge

Napier Railton. It was an unforgettable experience watching this giant of a car lapping the bumpy surface of the Brooklands oval at speeds of over a hundred miles an hour. Tom Levy's team used an old flat-bed lorry to transport whatever car was to compete, along with the ramps, spare parts, ropes, petrol and oil. As far as I can recall there were four of us. Tom, of course, was lord and master, then there was the chief fitter, his mate and, at the bottom of the heap, yours truly.

My first job, once the car had been manhandled off the lorry, was to get the polishing cloth going. After the first few trips I was trusted to check the tyres, oil and the chassis, to make certain that all the bolts were secured with split pins. All four of us had specific jobs. Whether the fitter and his mate ever got paid for what they were doing I haven't a clue. I only know that I never was, although I used to get small sums of cash for the little jobs I did for some of the other drivers. I tended to do the jobs nobody else wanted to do, like getting underneath the car to drain the hot oil, while at the same time scorching my clothes on the red-hot exhaust pipe.

In those days it only needed one nut to come adrift to cause a crash and, with no safety devices, like seat belts, a crash at Brooklands usually meant a stretcher job to the nearest mortuary. Luckily that never happened to us.

As far as I know Tom Levy never won much because his two MGs were the smallest of the MG marque so his only chance of a prize was in a handicap event. The MGs were only about 1100cc, unlike the Maseratis and the more modern English Racing Automobiles, or ERAs. ERA was a company formed by Humphrey Cook and Raymond Mays. Cook was the man with the money; his family ran a big firm of drapers. They wanted to design and build cars that could compete with the likes of Bugatti and Talbot. They were quite successful. Going back to Tom Levy, I suppose his vehicles were similar to the Austin Sevens and the Riley Nines, which was the well-respected car with which Freddie Dixon used to rule the roost. His main competitors were people like George Eyston and a Siamese driver of some fame, Prince Bira. All the bigger cars like the Talbots, the Alfas and, of course, the mighty Napier Railton charged around the infamous bumpy concrete bowl at breakneck speeds but it was always the Napier with John Cobb sitting dead upright at the wheel that won. If this mighty Goliath of a car hit a bump at a hundred miles an hour all four wheels took to the air. The crescendo of noise as they approached was tremendous, and then, as quick as a flash, they would disappear round the banking, leaving the strong and unmistakable smell of castor oil floating on the air. There was nothing like it. I became a sort of errand boy and general dogsbody at these meetings. 'Hey, Levy, where's that kid of yours?' was the signal for me to give a hand and get smothered in oil and grease – I loved it. To be given a ride around the track in some of the bigger cars, along with instructions to pump the oil whenever the pressure needle dropped below a certain figure, was a dream straight from heaven. A pair of overalls, smothered in grease and dirt and supplied by the boss, plus a black beret from one of the drivers – that was my uniform.

The first job when we got back to the garage was to lift the engine out of the chassis and set it up on a workbench ready for the fitter to get to work on it before the next meeting. This meant a complete strip down. Everything that moved either in a circle or up and down had to be cleaned, weighed and polished. The flywheel went to the engineering shop to be skimmed and balanced. This meant shaving metal off the wheel and it was not unusual to skim as much as half an inch off its width. The finishing touch would be a polish job. The same attention was paid to the con rods and the cam followers. The inside of the exhaust and inlet valve channels also had to be polished: no obstruction to the flow was the name of the game. Those engines of the twenties and thirties, whether amateur or works' run, were objects of industrial beauty.

Nearly all the drivers at meetings in those days had independent means of some sort. I don't know how they behaved towards men of my class when they met us in ordinary life – probably 'Do this, my man' or something similar – but on the track it was another matter. I was never talked down to because I was the 'Levy kid'. During the meetings it wasn't unusual for the whole family of an aspiring driver to be sitting at tables in the pits, while a butler waited on them with dainty sandwiches and flowing champagne, especially after a win.

I once witnessed a tragedy which gave me an insight into the way these elite people hid their emotions. It was at the Brooklands Easter meeting, the opening meet of the year. One young scion, attempting to overtake on, of all places, the Byfleet banking, came adrift and shot over the edge of the track. The result was flames, smoke and one very dead driver. A couple of labourers were sent with a stretcher to bring the remains of the lad back to the pits while the family went on supping the champagne with very few apparent signs of grief. On the way home the crew talked about the crash. Tom Levy said, 'That's what they're like, some of them seem not to have emotions, not like us.'

Tom Levy was never really 'one of them'. First of all, he worked for a living, but, more importantly, he was Jewish. All the same, a lot of 'them' were his friends.

I was now beginning to exhibit the behaviour patterns that I would show all my life. Once I got used to a job I lost interest, packed it in and looked for fresh pastures and more money. I was still only earning fifteen shillings a week, not enough. As well as which, girls were entering my field of vision.

22

Peggy

As we got older we began to see more of the girls and the sexual divide slowly began to close – this was usually because the girls took the lead. In my case it was a simple approach. There was a café around the corner from Kenton Street in Marchmont Street where a bunch of us spent our evenings nattering about the events of the day (that's when we weren't in Soho earning a bob or two). Without any warning this girl – her name was Peggy – who I had known since we were tiny, came across to me, put her arm through mine and without any emotion or bashfulness announced to all and sundry that 'Vic and I are going for a walk up West'. That was it: by that simple action Peggy had announced that from now on I was her property and at the same time warned off any of her friends who might have designs on my body. I didn't want any of my mates to think that I was some sort of a pansy, so I fell in with the idea. After all, Peggy was one of the better looking local girls and, not only that, she had just proved herself to be someone not to mess with.

My grandparents who took us in when Father left.

Uncles and aunts on the Hamblin side of the family. My mother is far left and my grandmother far right.

When I was six I was taken into care by the Salvation Army and placed in the Shaftesbury Home for Boys. We were fed, clothed and exercised.

Our local policeman looked just like this. Nicknamed 'the Bear', he kept a fatherly eye on all us kids.

The home was run along military lines. I think the idea was to prepare us for the Royal Navy.

Like the boys in this picture, we had an enlightened headmaster at Cromer Street School, Mr Thornton, who made sure that we learned more than the Three 'R's.

A lot of lads saw boxing as a way out of poverty.

This is where I knocked a lad out defending my sister's honour. The flats were once a slum, but the kids I met there recently live in a different world to the one I grew up in.

King's Cross Station, where we used to steal coal and get chased off by the police.

Covent Garden Market, where as kids we scrounged veg, and where later I worked and did a lot of growing up.

Within two years of this picture, John Cobb, driver of this car, the mighty Naipier Railton, would be in the RAF fighting the Luftewaffe. When I was fifteen I used to get taken round the track in it, squeezed into the cockpit.

The very same car, with its twenty four litre engine, is still going strong today.

Charles Laughton, the famous actor, used to hire me to wash up at his parties.

Then, as now, Soho was known for ladies of the night. Their pimps hired us to watch out for the law.

Musicians looking for work gather in Archer Street. When I was a teenager it was part of my Soho stamping ground.

The two guitarists in the centre are Stephane Grappelli and Django Reinhardt, my musical heroes.

We hung around and drank beer in places like this, unaware that before long our world was about to change for ever.

Oswald Mosley and his Blackshirts tried to stir up hatred against our Jewish neighbours. When I was seventeen we fought him and his mob in the Battle of Sidmouth Street. He didn't come back.

Me, a newly enlisted Rifleman, ready to take on the world. My apprenticeship in King's Cross is over. I am off to learn a new skill – the art of war.

The pair of us were almost the same age, but at fifteen Peggy was an almost fully developed young lady whose hormones were telling her that kissing a boy was only the start of things. As a young man I had none of these urges. I was more interested in whether Spurs were going to pulverise Arsenal next time they met, and how I was going to raise the cash to order one of those flash new suits from Harry Rubinstein's tailor's shop up the Cally. So Peggy, for all of her famous fighting spirit, had a job on her hands.

For instance, one time I arranged to meet her to go to the pictures. This was a special date and we were going to the Dominion on the corner of Tottenham Court Road and New Oxford Street. Unfortunately one of my mates from Harrison Street had come up with a bunch of tickets for a punch-up at the Ring, the famous boxing pub in Blackfriars. There was no competition. Peggy slipped my mind completely. Two days later and there was Peggy crying her eyes out; one of her mates came up and told me what a right sod I was. When I took her arm to say how sorry I was (a complete lie) she went into spasms of woe. Then suddenly, without warning, she lost her pathetic 'little girl lost' look and became a kind of Boadicea, a warrior type. She was fearsome in her attack on men in general and me in particular. I was lost. I didn't have a clue what all the shouting was about but we eventually made it up. Peggy lived in Cromer Street and I used to take her for strolls around Holborn and Soho and into the classier cafés, which really impressed her. 'How do you know all these people, Vic?' My mum kept on about me bringing her up for a visit. 'When are we going to meet this nice girl I saw you with the other day?'

Peggy and I were children of King's Cross; we had everything in common, we had grown up together on the same streets and our families lived in similar circumstance, everyone crammed into two rooms. Peg's family were, if anything, worse off. There was no way either of us could put on airs and graces. Peggy was well aware of the sort of boys I mixed with, and she also knew that I was what was called 'a safe pair of hands', which meant I was one of the boys who could handle themselves.

My main embarrassment was that my sister, little Emmy, who was now nine, kept Mum and Gran fully informed as to what was happening with 'Vic's girlfriend', and of course they were eager to know how things were shaping up. 'Might make yer more responsible to other people' was my gran's line.

Peggy was determined to nail me and to live happily ever after with roses round the door, which was what we reckoned all the girls spent their time planning. Of course they were nice to look at and sometimes walk around with, but we knew we should never let them get the whip hand which was easier said than done.

One evening she decided we were going for a walk up West. I took her round to one of the cafés I knew in Greek Street where I was in good with the Italian couple who ran it. This was because some of the lads from Sidmouth Street had seen off a small bunch of youths who had started to smash the café up. Normally we wouldn't have got involved, but one of the lads in our gang was Italian. We had been sitting there supping up and nattering among ourselves when this group barged in. When one of them started pushing around the old lady who ran the place, our Italian mate saw red and waded in. We followed him and there was an almighty punch-up which ended with us winning the day. Since then we had always been welcome, which was why I was now sitting there with my Peggy, telling her that she could have anything she fancied on the menu, knowing full well that it would cost me next to nothing, perhaps nothing at all.

Peggy probably wondered where on earth I had got the money to take her to this posh restaurant in the West End, although really it was an upmarket café. I let her think on. 'You know what, Peg, when you're with all your friends, what do they think of you running after me like you do?' 'Oh, they're like little kids, all they want to know is have we "done it yet".' 'Well, what do you tell 'em?' 'I just say that you're not like the other boys. I'm going to be a virgin when we get married.' So then I said, 'Let's get one thing straight, Peg, I'm not getting married till I've made my fortune. I ain't gonna take no wife into the sort of life that we've been brought up in.'

So there we were, a couple of fifteen-year-olds chatting away about the road to married bliss and all that went with it. I'm certain that dear Peggy knew exactly what she was talking about, but to me it was cissy talk – women, girls, marriage, babies. I thought that girls and their ambitions were dangerous to have around. But how do you get rid of them, and if you do discover the magic formula that undoes the chains, what do you replace them with? But I enjoyed sitting in that café, listening to a nice looker prattling on. Being in her company certainly made me feel good and I was well aware that there was hardly a boy in the neighbourhood who wouldn't have liked to get his hands in her knickers. In spite of all this, and my physical attraction towards her, I managed to control myself, much to Peggy's disappointment. I couldn't forget the misery that my mum had suffered over my dad, and in some strange way a bit of me blamed the institution of marriage. Not that I spent all that much time thinking about these things. I had more important things on my mind, like how to make a fortune.

23

Jobs and Sods

M y next job was as a pastry cook's assistant, in a small bread shop in Tavistock Place, next door to home. Gran had noticed the advert for a 'smart youth' in the shop window and had promptly marched in and told them that the 'smart youth' would be on the doorstep the next day. It's true she knew that I was once again 'on the stones', as we called being out of work, but she was still taking a chance saying I would be there. Gran never did things by halves; when I arrived home that evening I was greeted by the words: 'Got a job yet, Victor?' 'Not yet, Gran.' 'Start tomorrow morning at the Tavistock Bakery, one pound a week and all the bread you can bring home. And before you leave this house in the morning I want to see you clean and tidy, not your usual scruffy self!'

The bakery was staffed by a pastry cook, a chef, an under-chef and a chap of about eighteen who was working as an apprentice. Then, last of all, me, the dogsbody, as usual.

I had to do all the jobs that the other three considered below their status, like cleaning the floors. Once a week I had to get on my hands and knees and scrape away at the concrete to remove all the dried flour and paste which got brushed off the work tables. By the end of the week all the debris had been so stamped and trodden in that it had become an inch-thick coating on top of the concrete, forming a sort of carpet. The Tavistock Bakery was reckoned to be the finest bakehouse in all Bloomsbury, so what the worst one must have been like boggles the mind. Nothing was thrown away. The sugar, for instance, was measured from a huge sack that stood in the corner. On a shelf next to the mixing board there was a large, square biscuit tin. It was the custom to empty any excess sugar, wherever it came from, and that included the floor, into 'the biscuit tin'. It was this second-hand sugar that they used to coat the doughnuts and other cakes.

The under-chef was a Scot, a short, stocky individual who looked like he had served his apprenticeship in the boxing ring at Blackfriars. His chosen sport was cross-country running and he eventually succeeded in persuading me to join him on his training runs, three times round the Outer Circle in Regent's Park, which he did three evenings a week. His name was Robert but because he was Scottish we knew him as 'Bruce'. It was Bruce who introduced me to the Marlborough Athletics Club in Drury Lane and for the first time since leaving school I began to enjoy going to work, not because of the job itself, which I hated, but the spirit that prevailed between the four of us and especially being invited to take part in the training schedules, which really lifted me.

It was in this job that I first got a real inkling about sex. The chef used to bang away at the shop manageress most afternoons, while his mate was to be found in a cupboard servicing one of the shop girls. It was all quite open.

This job lasted until one day when I was talking to Bruce. I don't remember how it came up but in the heat of the moment I called him a 'Scotch bastard'. He let fly at me with the big wooden shovel that was used to draw the cakes out of the oven. After both he and the cakes had cooled down, he said he was quite sorry it had happened, but it did teach me never to call anyone a bastard unless I was prepared to go to war. In fact, I have never used the term since, at least not in the same personal way, but that was it. Another job down the drain and yet another question and answer session with our gran who insisted that I had disgraced the family. ''Ow am I expected to show my face in that shop again?' The diatribe was relentless and well justified although I didn't think so at the time. It did cross my mind that Gran was upset because she realised that there would be no more free bread and cakes.

My next attempt to make my fortune was as an assistant packer at Rose Brothers, a cloth warehouse in New Oxford Street which supplied all the local sweatshops with their fabrics. It was while working here helping the delivery driver that I got an insight into the hard work my mum did in order to put a crust on the table.

All over the area that lay between Tottenham Court Road, Mortimer Street and Great Portland Street there were dozens of small dressmaking and milliners' shops, all competing with one another for the lucrative West End fashion trade. They were nearly all Jewish-owned. The girls and women were intensely loyal to whoever they were working for. In her time, Mother must have done a stint at every milliner's workshop in the district. The girls followed the work and they all understood why they might be laid off by Mr Rubenstein one day and taken on the next by his rival, Mr Knosher. Mr Knosher would put in a price for a line of hats, then Mr Rubenstein would put in a lower price and get the work. So Mr Knosher laid a dozen off and Mr Rubenstein took them on. The employers of these highly skilled women knew that, whatever happened, they had to keep them in the district.

I soon got bored stiff with the brothers Rose, so I took a job as a humble delivery boy for a grocer in Marchmont Street. It was there that I had my first brush with the law. I got done for dangerous driving while demonstrating to all the world how easy it was to drive a three-wheeled box tricycle not on three wheels but two. That cost me five bob at Clerkenwell Magistrates' Court.

There were repercussions. More than twenty-five years later I applied for a job with London Transport as a bus driver and had to go to the Carriage Office in Vauxhall to get my PSV licence. One of the questions on the form was about past convictions. Naturally I had long ago forgotten about the tricycle incident, but the police hadn't and my application was returned as being inaccurate. I was completely at a loss to know why; they told me to think back but for the life of me I couldn't remember doing anything wrong, so finally they told me. It goes to prove that they've got you down from the cradle to the grave.

24

Bloomsbury Society

The job at the grocer's in Holborn was only ten minutes' walk from the wretchedness of Sidmouth Street and Harrison Street but it was like being transported to another planet.

The streets in which we had played and grown up were solid working-class areas, where people worked for a pittance, the pubs carried on a roaring trade and it was a struggle just to survive. And, of course, in Holborn it was just as much a struggle as anywhere else, but blending in with it and floating right on the surface, in the middle and round the edges, was a volatile mix that made up the larger than life elements of Bloomsbury society.

Within the area between Russell and Gordon Squares, Gower Street, Museum Street and, of course, Bloomsbury Square itself, you found all sorts: poets, writers, arty-crafties, weirdy-beardies, folksy-wolksies, and every political creed under the sun.

At night the street girls took up their stations under their favourite lamp post or in a shop doorway ready to pounce on any passer-by who entered their territory. Us young kids earned money keeping these girls informed when the rozzers were about. For sixpence a week we kept watch and if we saw a copper we gave a signal and off the girls dashed to the nearest café or fish and chip shop to wait until we signalled that the coast was clear.

If the girls lasted a month without going before the local beak, we might be rewarded with a bonus of a shilling from the ponce who looked after their welfare. Not that there was much welfare in evidence, more likely a beating up if they failed to meet some target. But they were a carefree and happy group who accepted the rough life they led with a shrug, knowing that their position only lasted as long as their looks held out. When those started to go the next step was outside the railway stations of Paddington and King's Cross.

As well as dealing with the girls, the police kept an eye on the cafés that catered for the different political groups. They all had their own sacred venues. The most famous of these was the Red Book Club in Parton Street. The RBC was the home of the local communists and fellow travellers. The anarchists had a den in Red Lion Street, where their national paper was printed, while the Trots met up in a café in Museum Street. In those days the Labour Party had such a bad name that they had very little following except in the universities. As for the Tories, they were non-existent in the area.

As far as I can remember, no one was ever arrested; it was all fairly harmless stuff, and, far from being intimidated by the actions of the police, the harassment made these groups more vocal. These people could talk the hind legs off a donkey, so the altercations with the police often turned out to be very entertaining, though each political sect hated the other's guts.

Gradually I began to pick up on some of the arguments about the problems of that time: the growing strength of fascism in Europe, communism as the ultimate Garden of Eden, the Trots blasting away at anything that emanated from the soul of Stalin. The poets and the writers trying to find common ground and come up with an antidote, all of them, of course, failing in the end.

There was a lot of talk about Oswald Mosley and his Blackshirts. Mosley was the self-appointed head of the British Union of Fascists, an evil anti-Semitic crew. The Blackshirts used to go round the streets causing mayhem, breaking the windows of Jewish shopkeepers and putting the fear of God into anyone who opposed them. The worst thing about all this was the protection they had from the police. I knew that if a person or a group responded with force against these thugs it wasn't the Blackshirts who ended up in court the next morning.

For light entertainment we had the showgirls and the dancing boys, all living in the boarding houses that filled the streets round Russell Square. I never had a dull or uninteresting time during my life as a young resident of Bloomsbury, and I learnt more than I ever did at school.

One of the customers at the grocer's shop in Marchmont Street was Charles Laughton, the famous actor. He had a flat in Gordon Square. One day while I was delivering a basket of groceries to him, I came face to face with the great man himself. Would I care to earn some extra money, he asked. 'Not 'arf,' says I. 'Be here at seven sharp,' says he.

It turned out that he was holding a reception for some visitors from America. Part of my work was to wash the glasses and make myself useful to the cook. I earned myself a fiver that night. Laughton must have put it around to some of his cronies, because I was asked to do similar work quite a few times after that. I could only be contacted through Hales the Grocers so I was in the manager's good books for bringing in new custom.

At the time I was knocking around with a trio of lads who had left school at the same time as me. We liked hanging around Greek Street and Old Compton Street, in fact anywhere in Soho where we knew the sharp boys could be found. We performed small tasks in return for a 'floater', a sort of retainer of a couple of pounds a week, so we always had some extra money in our pockets. As the cliques got to know us we were given more difficult jobs like sussing out how long it took the local copper to do his beat and so on. Much later in life I learnt that this was termed 'aiding and abetting'. To us boys, however, it was all a bit of a lark and a way of earning a few bob on the side.

25

Running into Eddie Wilson

By now I was nearly sixteen, growing out my clothes like there was no tomorrow and for the umpteenth time I was out of work. I think my grandfather had given up on me. 'Pity you're not old enough to enlist, seven years in the army is what you need.' Mum and Gran were also at it. 'Victor, you got to settle down, learn a trade. In and out of work ain't no good for man or boy.' Pearls of wisdom, no doubt. 'OK, Mum, I promise to stick the next job I get.' I didn't even have my tongue in my cheek. I suppose I must have meant it at the time.

One day, by a stroke of luck, I met up with a character who remembered me from my visits to Brooklands. I was strolling along Great Portland Street, in those days home to specialist sports car manufacturers. Frazer Nash had a dealership along with Salmson and other well-known marques. Eddie Wilson recognised me from the other side of the road and hailed me. Eddie owned a small garage in Chiswick High Road which specialised in converting small-engine-capacity cars into sports models. I explained how I came to be strolling about in the middle of the day when I should have been hard at it earning a crust and he offered me a job.

'The money's not great but the work is interesting, take it as a type of apprenticeship.' So I started my tenth job in two years.

Grandfather softened up and took me around to a second-hand bike shop and bought me a bike for ten shillings. 'Can't afford bus fares and the exercise will do you good.' Mum and Gran were also well pleased.

Eddie Wilson was spot-on when he said that the money was rotten, but this was because he and his two mates valued their freedom. Eddie's motto was 'I'd rather live on cheese sandwiches than work for wages'. The firm's income came mostly from the orders it got from sports conversions plus the occasional odd jobs that found their way in via the back door, when some crooked dealer needed Eddie's skill at altering the bodywork of a stolen car so that even its former owner would never recognise it.

Eddie had a contact who used to pop into the shop twice a week to ask him what he was going to need for the next week. Eddie gave him a list and a couple of days later the goods appeared. Everything needed was acquired bent, 'to keep costs down'.

As usual I was on the bottom rung of the hierarchy so all the dirty and boring jobs came my way. A customer might bring in an old clapped-out Austin Seven, Morris Eight, Ford Ten or any car that we used to call a 'light car'. The team immediately set to work stripping away all the bodywork, which was then dumped in the backyard. The next bit of the operation was to remove all ancillary parts until the chassis was laid bare on the long bench and then it was my job to clean off all the rust and grime with a wire brush, then emery paper and, finally, a degreaser. Next I put on a coat of primer and when that was dry a second and third coat. Then the painter came in and applied the finish, usually a bright-red high gloss. As soon as the chassis was done I could start on the axles, springs and all the other parts that had to be bolted on before the new bodywork arrived. This was all made out of aluminium sheets and made by one of Eddie's mates. The body had to be screwed and bolted to wooden struts which were made of seasoned ash. The engines were supplied by the customer and so long as the chassis was strong enough any engine could be used.

Eddie and his mates were true craftsmen but the work took a lot of man hours, and while the finished product was a work of great precision the numbers of sports car enthusiasts who could afford it were few. There were occasional visits from the law, but they never came to anything and were just part of the game. So for the second time since leaving school I felt good about going to work in the morning. Eddie taught me the importance of getting things right. 'If they have to bring a car back, Vicky boy, you can safely say you've lost a customer.' Eddie's light cars may have started life as a load of rubbish but by the time they had been through his hands the rubbish had been turned into a work of art.

Peggy, meanwhile, was still hanging on and still a virgin. She and I used to take long walks together in the evenings. I

can't remember what we talked about but I know that she
had feelings of which I knew nothing. Her hints that 'I could
do what I liked' hit a blank wall, so finally Peggy decided that
she was wasting her time and gave me the boot. She began to
transfer her affections to a tall ginger-haired chap.

26

. . . and Fred

My grandfather seemed to have given up on me (even if he'd softened up a bit when I started working for Eddie), my mum thought I was going to be a famous violinist, my gran had her doubts and said that I would probably end up as a jack of all trades and master of none: myself, I wasn't too certain of things.

It was one of those cold and blustery evenings, pelting down cats and dogs outside, typical English February, and I was giving my granddad a hand. One of his hobbies was keeping God happy by printing the monthly hymn sheets for the local church. I used to help by placing the sheets on to a metal plate while the old man operated a handle which sent the inked rollers over the sheet. Then I had to remove the sheet and put in a new one. Helping him like this saved grandfather a whole load of time and effort and I know he appreciated it. He had once offered me extra pocket money to do this little chore but I had refused it and my gran later told me that he never forgot that episode. That was why he never completely gave up on me – goes to show that little things mean a lot.

Anyway, when we had finished Gran said to me: 'Victor, go round to the fish and chip shop and we'll all have a nice supper.' 'It's pouring with rain, Gran.' 'Take the umbrella, then, four tuppennies and a pennorth and a piece of fourpenny skate for Granddad.' Which meant that Granddad was going to get a nice big piece of skate, while us lesser members of the household would get a helping of so-called 'rock salmon', in those days the lowest of the low. Out into the cold and rain I went, en route for Leigh Street which was a turning off Marchmont Street, about a thousand yards or so, no big deal,.

As was usual on a Friday the fish shop was full to bursting. 'Hello, Vic.' I gets a dig in the ribs and I turns round to face the foe. 'Hello, Fred, 'aven't seen you for years.' Fred was the chap I had the bust-up with when I first went to Cromer Street School. 'Keeping going, yer know, a bit of this and a bit of that.' 'Nuffink regular, then?' 'No, but I have got something going that could interest you.' If Fred said he was doing a 'bit of this and a bit of that' it meant only one thing: up a drainpipe one night, in through a basement window the next.

But I was wrong. 'You still keeping up with that violin playing you was so good at when we were at school?' 'Not really, Fred, get it down now and again, no time to practise.' Fred carried on. 'There's four of us, we got a little band together, you remember Joe Brown, he's got hold of one of them new mini pianas, we've got two other blokes, one is a

130

drummer, got his own drums and a clarinet player. I play the trumpet.' By now we'd lost our place in the queue. 'I tell yer what, Vic, come down to the Tonbridge on Wednesday at seven, we need someone who can write down music, don't forget, next Wednesday.' When I finally got home with the supper, 'Thought you'd fallen down a drain hole, you've been an hour.' 'Sorry, Gran, the queue was awful big.'

My last encounter with Fred Munday had been quite bloody but here he was four years later greeting me like an old friend. So the upshot of it was that I turned up at the Tonbridge Club the following Wednesday night and my next little adventure began.

27

Joe Brown's Masters of Rhythm

The arrival of De Hot Club de King's Cross and Joe Brown's Masters of Rhythm:

Joe Brown	leader and piano
Fred Munday	trumpet
Roscoe Barnato	clarinet
Smudger Smith	drums
Vic Gregg	violin and arranger

I arrived just after seven. Directly I set eyes on Joe Brown I remembered him from years before, but now, instead of the rundown appearance he used to have, he was togged out in the latest gear, with his hair smoothed down as if it had been ironed into place. Joe had charted the course he was going to take: he was going to be a bandleader, so he started a band – Joe Brown's Masters of Rhythm. I didn't know the other two lads. Joe introduced me, then said, 'Get yer fiddle out and let's see if you can fit in.' He sat down at the piano and began bashing away at 'I'm Nobody's Sweetheart Now', a well-known number that had been around since the twenties. Then I realised what was going on: Joe was laying it on in C major, while Fred and the lad with the clarinet wanted B flat. As for me, it didn't make any difference what key they played in. I could cope, but not so the wood and the trumpet. Joe stopped playing and asked me, 'What you think, Vic?' I had to lay it on the line: if he wanted to play piano he had to learn his scales. C major was for the birds.

It appeared that the mini piano had come into Joe's hands because of a painting job he had done for a local pawnbroker who gave him the piano rather than part with any cash. Fred and the other lad had also acquired their instruments via a pawnshop and, to learn their musical skills, Fred and this lad, whose name was Roscoe, and who was Jewish, became members of the Salvation Army band. Twice a week they were expected to play their part outside the local pubs while the female stalwarts of the Army went around with the hat. Roscoe's Jewishness never caused the Sally Army any concern. As for Roscoe himself, he just said, 'So I'm a Jewboy, so what, anybody want to make somefink of it?' Roscoe was known for being able to handle himself so nobody wanted to 'make somefink of it'.

Surprising as it was, our little band gradually improved. Roscoe's Mum and Dad supplied us with an old wind-up gramophone and we used to go down to Woolies (Woolworths) and buy the latest records at sixpence a time. I wrote out a simple one-line score on the special paper that Fred or Roscoe managed to lift from the practice rooms of the Sally.

Now Joe had to learn to play the keyboard better and also to read a score. It said much for his dedication that inside a month he could place his fingers on the notes exactly as I had written them. I can also remember that the lad who had the drums was called Smudger, and he was the only one of us who had no problems: he had a natural bent for rhythm. It was Smudger who made sure we kept to the tempo.

After a couple of months it was decided that there was no way that Joe could be our pianist, so it was agreed that he would be in charge and run things. So we had a bandleader who knew nothing about the complexities of music, couldn't play an instrument but was as keen as mustard, as in fact we all were – it was infectious.

Meanwhile, I was having my usual problems on the work front. Eddie Wilson told me the firm was going bust for lack of orders, so I acted the gentleman and jacked it in. Eddie gave me my cards and put in a good word for me at the labour exchange. I was on the stones again. So up to Penton Street once more where they fixed me up with a job as a junior mechanic with Pickford's Transport. They had a big garage halfway along the City Road, which was no problem seeing that my bike was still in running order. I was now earning twenty-five shillings a week, a step up in the world, and as well as this there was the band. The garage at City Road was a huge affair. Already in situ were two lads I knew from Cromer Street, but because of Eddie's reference the firm had accepted me as a junior mechanic which was a cut above the other two, who were only labourers on a 'oncer' (a pound) a week. Anyone who read the bull that Eddie had put into my reference would think that I could build any vehicle from a basket job to a market leader. When the foreman in charge discovered that I had no tools he rightly marked me down as 'useful but don't put him in charge of rebuilding a braking system'.

I never dropped any clangers and, week by week, I earned my twenty-five bob without any trouble. Start at eight, finish at five, keep my nose clean and you've got a job for life, thus spake the foreman. If only.

Meanwhile, back to De Hot Club de King's Cross.

Some weeks after we had settled into the small basement room at the Tonbridge Club, Fred brought along the big chief from the Salvation Army's place in Judd Street, plus the chief's wife, who introduced herself as Sister Evelyn but told us it would not be seen as rude if we just called her Sister Evie. This dedicated couple, dressed in their regulation Sally Army uniform, him with his gold-braided military cap and Evie with her bonnet complete with ribbon sitting neatly on the back of her head, had come along to see how their two protégés were getting on with the band that Fred had told them about. The upshot was that we were offered the use of the Salvation Army's practice room for up to six hours a week spread over two evenings, nothing later than eight o'clock.

Sister Evie took one look at Joe's clapped-out mini piano and suggested that we could leave it where it was as there was a nice piano already in the Sally's room. If there was a boss of the outfit, it was Evie. She was very interested when she learnt that I was doing the arranging. 'But, Victor, why no bass clef?' 'Well, Sister, we don't ever go down that low.' This seemed to satisfy her. What I didn't explain was that if I started messing around with bass clefs I would be the only one of us who could understand what it was all about. If the good sister had been given a taste of our repertoire it is unlikely that we'd have been allowed within a mile of the cherished practice room.

So we offered our profuse thanks to the chap who ran the day-to-day business of the Tonbridge Club and went over to the other side of the street to the Salvation Army's big, solidly built corner establishment.

Joe brought along a couple of records by Django Reinhardt and Stéphane Grappelli and was super-keen to get us doing the jazz thing. 'There's only five of them in the Reinhardt band, should be a cakewalk, they 'aven't even got a joanna.' It seemed simple to Joe, who always looked for the easy way if anything had to be done. 'Yes, but Joe they do have a string bass and two guitars, we've got a trumpet, a drummer and a clarinet, what we need is a bass player.' Anyway we all agreed that if we could find a way to make it work then we would be the local kings of jazz. So we practised and practised again and again and again and then, all of a sudden, both Fred and myself and Roscoe discovered that things were falling into place. Sister Evie even presented Joe with an old conductor's baton which he wielded with enthusiasm.

She turned out to be our fairy godmother. When she discovered that our bandleader couldn't play a note she came up with an old acoustic guitar. 'I will arrange for you to have lessons, Joe, leave it to me.' Within a month Joe was sitting in strumming the chords like a real old hand. This was good because we all sensed that Joe had been on the point of giving up; we were getting better while he was standing still. Now the hours flew by, and the Masters of Rhythm were taking shape.

Joe came in to the Tuesday practice one day with the news that we had been asked to play at the Saturday evening dance at the Tonbridge, and what did we all reckon?

Meanwhile, out on the street dear Peggy had been having second thoughts about Gingernut and decided to reclaim her property. She had heard about the new band and that we were playing all the latest numbers. What with Joe and Smudger strolling round the local manor with their brand new sharp suits, and hair all shiny with the latest grease known as Brilliantine, they looked the business and the girls were attracted to us like moths to a flame.

While we were packing up our gear after finishing the evening practice, which included chatting up the girls, Peggy suggested we 'go for a stroll'. 'What, at eleven o'clock at night?' 'I want to, Vic.' That was it, I was suckered, so we started going out once again. 'I didn't think you loved me any more,' said Peggy, laying it on thick and heavy. 'What made you change your mind?' I replied, sensing that now I held the whip hand. Peggy came back with 'My mum said you must be a good man, she asked me if you had ever tried it on and I told her that you wasn't the type to do that. My mum said that she wished she had met a boy like you when she was young, and Daisy likes you as well.' Daisy was Peggy's younger sister and reckoned to be a bit of a stunner.

Peggy was well aware of the unwritten code of conduct – we had announced our pairing, or at least Peggy had – so if I dumped her now without good reason I would be thought of as someone not to be trusted, so I couldn't give her the brush-off without a good excuse. I was hooked and all it needed now was for her to reel in the line.

One day in the summer, after we had enjoyed an evening at the Tatler News Cinema in Charing Cross Road, I took her into a little restaurant I knew just off of Greek Street. I asked if she enjoyed the meal. 'I didn't know that you could afford to come to a place like this, Vic. If you did it to impress me then you wasted your money. What you spent here should 'ave been put into the bank.' 'What for?' says I. 'It's easy to earn a couple of bob round here.' 'Well, don't you ever think about the future? Sooner or later we will get married and we will have to buy furniture and all sorts of stuff.'

Well, there it was. Peggy had tied the message to the mast for all to see, and I couldn't summon up the courage to tell her that getting married was indeed for the future – the very distant future. I was happy and proud enough to be in her company, but getting married? Marriage was for old people and nutcases. My bacon was saved by the advent of the ginger-headed nutter himself. It was during one of our practice sessions, the room was full and along with the band there was the usual crowd of girls and some of our mates. The air was full of tobacco smoke. Smudger's continual thumping of the pedal on his bass drum added to the general air of youthful exuberance. The hubbub slowly died down as a tall, ginger-headed geezer with two well-built muscle men came into the room and made his way over to the band. He started laying down the law about me messing with his girl. Apparently Peggy had gone on seeing him while she was seeing me. Roscoe, seeing that I was in trouble, picked up the leg of a broken chair and poked it in front of the lad's nose.

The trio were outnumbered and beat a hasty retreat. Peggy must have been impressed by her new lover's determination, because she decided that, for better or worse, the new boy was the best bet. It wouldn't be long before she was up the spout and walking up the aisle, her childhood over.

28

Saturday Night Dance Halls

Now that I had a steady job and a place in the band my life was beginning to settle down. I was giving more money to Mum and I still had a couple of bob in my pocket. Brother John was toiling away as a delivery boy in a grocer's shop in Pulteney Street Market. Mum was certain that I would become famous, and my grandparents both agreed that at last I had got my head straight. But if there was one thing that exercised its pull over us all it had to be the local Saturday dance hall. This was the rendezvous where girls met boys and vice versa, liaisons were made and most of the girls decided who was going to be their future husband and the father of their children.

The young men may well have had the filthiest of occupations throughout the working week but, come Friday night, preparations started for the Saturday night dance. Sisters or mothers were cajoled into putting a knife-edge crease in the trousers, the latest fancy tie was smoothed and ironed, out came the shiny cufflinks, the patent leather pointed shoes were buffed up and the soles of the shoes rubbed down with fine glass paper so that the dancer could exhibit his dexterity and slide over the highly polished dance floors. Before entering the hall the lads gathered together to chat about the better points of the girls they hoped to dazzle and what their techniques were going to be. The girls were already in position watching the boys as they came in and had been practising the latest steps all week with the aid of the gramophones in their bedrooms. The girls had it all worked out: they knew which of the opposite sex could carry them around the floor without mishap, the clumsy ones who couldn't dance a step, the ones they fancied and the ones they wouldn't be seen dead with. Then there was the band itself. It was fashionable for the band to be dressed in the same style. All their jackets were the same colour as were the bow ties, the trousers immaculately creased and the hair plastered down with the latest scented grease. If there was ever a cult figure it had to be the leader of the local dance band; he was the real star of the evening and that was what our mate Joe Brown wanted to be.

We had about three weeks to prepare for our debut. The Sally Army bandmaster sat in on one of our practice evenings and decided we needed help. He made us understand the need for a repertoire and taught us the importance of practice, a bar at a time. He gave Joe confidence by telling him that he didn't have to be able to read music; his job was to keep order, keep to a strict tempo and to impose his authority by whacking us with the baton if and when we got out of line. 'Where did you get that twig, Joe?' says the bandmaster, pointing to Joe's treasured baton. 'Sister Evie gave it to me.' The bandmaster disappeared and came back with a stick similar to the canes we had known at school. 'This will do you far better than that flimsy thing,' he says to Joe. 'Just give them a whack every now and again. Even if they don't deserve it whack them all the same.' To Joe's credit he ignored that particular pearl of wisdom.

Finally, the great day arrived: our debut in the world of dance music. What saved us was the insistence of 'the General', as we called the bandmaster, on the importance of tempo. If you're playing music to dance to then keeping the correct time is more important than hitting the right notes. The General knew a thing or two about dance bands. Thanks to him we now had a repertoire of about thirty songs which I shuffled around for the next six weeks as the resident band of the Tonbridge Club. The General and his wife kept our noses to the grindstone. We knew that none of us would ever be able to match the dexterity of Django Reinhardt and his sidekick Stéphane Grappelli, but you can't say we didn't try.

The Tonbridge Club with its Saturday night dances became a beacon for the boys and girls of the neighbourhood. Then another crony from my childhood past turned up to join in the mêlée that was the small square dance floor at the club.

29

Defending Sidmouth Street

I had known Eddie Mathews since my earliest days at infants' school. Eddie had always been one of the scruffiest of the scruffs, a prime example of the kids who came out of the hovels of Sidmouth Street, but here was Eddie in a well-tailored suit, flash tie and a pair of shiny shoes on his feet that would have put Fred Astaire to shame, walking in to one of the Saturday night hops at the Tonbridge with a couple of his mates in tow, both equally shined up.

The girls immediately started fiddling with their make-up. In no time at all the music came to a stop and there we all were shaking hands and remarking how well we were all looking. Less than three years ago we'd been knocking each other's blocks off. So it ended up with me and Eddie chatting away in a corner of the hall. It turned out that Eddie was part of a small gang that got its living by doing a bit of breaking and entering, mainly small shops and offices up West. They'd got a dealer in Somers Town that took anything worthwhile and if they could manage two decent capers a week it was better than working for wages. 'What you think, Vic? If you're interested, you're in.' Eddie knew it was safe to confide in me; he remembered me as one of the gang. I was up there with the best of them. I told him I would think about it, which really meant that I was beginning to tire of my 'safe' job at Pickford's and was ready for pastures new. Did I know anything about acetylene torches? This meant one thing only: safes. I told Eddie that I did indeed know how to operate a torch. When I met up with the gang for the second time, they said they had been told about an easy lift in some offices in Hatton Garden – uncut stones, no less, a real doddle. Not one of these potential number one villains had yet reached the age of seventeen. 'Working for wages is a mug's game, Vic, come and take a dekko at my motor.' Eddie showed me his Wolseley Ten. He wasn't eighteen yet so he'd taxed it in his dad's name. 'Fink about it, Vic.'

In the meantime our tenure at the Tonbridge Club was coming to an end, as were the days of the small-time dance halls. In their place, huge, glamorous Palais de Danse were springing up all over London, with their magnificent floors and the glitz and dazzle of the modern décor, and big-name bands. Saturday night at the Palais was the place to be seen strutting your stuff and making it with the impressive array of skirt that was always on parade. The Hot Club de King's Cross was about to pass into history. Joe tried his utmost to keep us together but in spite of our energy and keenness we just weren't good enough. Joe Brown's Masters of Rhythm slipped into history and nobody missed us.

Discord between husband and wife was such a common occurrence that normally little notice was taken of a family bust-up. Sometimes a neighbour might shout out of a window telling the perpetrators to 'Knock it off, you two', or something less politely worded and more to the point.

One young couple who lived two doors away from us and up on the second floor were going at it hammer and tongs. When the girl started screaming the neighbours sensed that this was no ordinary marital dispute. Suddenly the screaming stopped. The small crowd which had gathered in the street below was beginning to disperse when there was a terrific crash as the girl hurled herself out of the window to smash, a couple of seconds later, on to the pavement below.

The ambulance from the station in Herbrand Street, just around the corner, was on the scene in minutes, closely followed by a police van. The law took the struggling young husband away to the cells in Judd Street and next day we learnt that their little girl had been taken into care.

Family fights were a daily occurrence, but women didn't usually throw themselves out of windows. The favoured way of exiting the wretchedness of life in the slums of King's Cross was to shut all the doors and windows, turn on the gas tap, place a pillow on the lowered door of the gas oven and go to sleep.

The second tragedy to hit the street came some weeks after the death of the young woman. The street woke to find the police had formed a cordon around one of the dwellings. In it a wife and the three young children had been discovered in a roomful of blood. Their throats had been cut while they slept. The husband had scarpered and had yet to be found. I think both these two tragic events had a very strong effect on me and on the decisions I was about to make.

Eddie came round to see me again and told me he was very keen about my using the acetylene torch. I offered to have a look at it for him and discovered that he had no oxygen bottle to go with it and didn't even know one was necessary. I told him to get someone to lift a full bottle from the engineer's yard at the back of Euston Station: 'They just leave 'em lying around, they wheel them round in pairs fixed to a trolley so you'll have to nick two together. Let me know when you've got the gear.' Eddie gave me a slap on the back. 'I knew you'd see sense at last, Vic.'

Eddie didn't understand that while I was willing to give him the info about getting the oxygen I was going to steer clear of becoming involved in any more criminal adventures. I finished up giving him and his mates the lowdown on using the acetylene but turned down Eddie's offer of taking part in 'a nice little earner', as he put it. In the end he and his two mates managed to lay their hands on the oxygen bottle but then discovered it was going to take a much larger team to carry out their diamond caper. It seemed to me that three teenagers with no organisational skills were on a hiding to nothing. And I was right: within six months Eddie and his gang were doing a stretch in Brixton Prison and in those days if you were handed a five-year stretch then that is what you served.

As we got older the influence of our street gangs began to wane. We were all going our own separate ways, forming new attachments and taking on jobs that took us out of the area. Mixing with girls no longer marked you out as a cissy.

We never lost our suspicion of authority and this was made worse by the things that were happening around us.

Mosley's fascist party was making big trouble. In the poorer areas of London, the East End and south of the river, ordinary people were divided into those who had work and those who hadn't. Those with work were, on the whole, anti-fascist; men on the dole, on the other hand, followed the Mosley line that it was all the fault of the Jews and immigrants. The fighting in the streets changed; it was no longer gangs bashing each other up for the fun of it. Mosley was stirring things up and the result was racial hatred.

One Saturday morning in late March I was in one of the local cafés in Gray's Inn Road, run by a man called Frankie, whose real name wasn't actually Frank but Franz. He was a German ex-prisoner of war and had met and married a girl from King's Cross. They'd run the café from as long as us lads could remember; the old man wanted to call the café after his son, also called Franz, but sensibly decided that 'Frankie's café' was better than 'Franz's café'.

Young Franz, also known as Frankie, was in our own age group.

It was the older Franz who first introduced the locals to frankfurters. His missus used to cook them in a large boiler in the backyard and the smell of the cooking sausages drifted through the neighbourhood with the result that the café was seldom empty.

There was more to the café's activities than supplying food and drink, however. It also provided a useful service to some of the local villains. In the distant past Franz senior had been apprenticed to a master jeweller, and any small trinkets that 'just happened to be left lying around' were taken in to the café, the stones removed and set to one side and the gold and silver melted down. Franz with his frankfurters and his little bit of fencing on the side was all right. He was one of us and a decent bloke, even if he was old enough to be our father.

I went into Frankie's one day to find Frankie junior and four of the lads deeply into a game of solo. The cash on the table indicated that this was a serious game. One of the players was Roscoe, the Jewboy clarinet player from our now forgotten dance band. Roscoe was moaning that the game was a fiddle while the other three were raking in their winnings. The game ended and Frankie had put a pot of tea on the table, with some bread rolls and half a dozen of those tasty frankfurters, and as we got stuck into the feast the four of them brought me up to date on what had been happening, especially an attack on Solly's greengrocery shop in Sidmouth Street. 'A gang of kids threw a brick through Solly's window yesterday.' Rozzie summed the situation up: 'We're waiting to see what happens next. We reckon that as there's two Jewboy shops next to each other a repeat performance is on the cards, in which case we're going to do the Blackshirts over good and proper.'

The two 'Jewboy shops' in question were Ruby Solomon's greengrocer shop and Bernie Morris's oil shop, actually opposite each other on the corners of Prospect Terrace and Sidmouth Street. The Solomons had two boys, who most of our lot had known since infants' school. The elder was nicknamed Solly but no one ever knew his real Christian name.

Solly he was and always would be. His younger brother was called Isaac and of course we called him Izzy. The pair of them were always together. Solly belonged to the local boxing club and modelled his style of fighting on that of the illustrious Jackie 'Kid' Berg, 'the Whitechapel Whirlwind'. Nobody messed with Solly: he was 'one of us'.

Ruby Solomon was the matriarch of the family and a lady of wide proportions. She sat out on her front steps and held court with all the other women at her end of Sidmouth Street. Everyone called her 'Mrs Ruby'. She feared neither man nor beast. More importantly, it was well known in the area that Ruby never refused a plea for 'something on the slate'. At the other end of the street was the redoubtable 'Auntie Elsie', a part-time midwife and sort of mother confessor. Auntie Elsie was yet another of that breed of woman who stood no nonsense from anybody. If by chance any Blackshirt gang did come around to create havoc then they would find that the wagons were circled against them. Inevitably, probably encouraged by the ease with which they had got away with the attack on the Solomons' shop, they came back for a second helping.

Roscoe and the crew he had gathered around him had been in the café since late morning; it was now late in the afternoon and they were on the point of calling the whole thing off. Then in dashed one of the small kids. 'There's a gang of 'em coming down from Swinton Street.' ''Ow many?' 'About a 'undred.' ''*Ow* many did you say?' 'Well, a lot of 'em.' By this time we could hear the racket they were making. I worked out that we had about twenty, top whack, nevertheless we kept to the plan: half down to the other end of the street, the other half to let the enemy pass and then close up the street and get them in the net.

As it turned out, and luckily for us, there weren't a hundred of them or anything like. The actual force was about ten of the hard nuts with the usual complement of onlookers and do-nothing supporters. In no time the Blackshirts (they were actually wearing their uniform) were herded together and pushed and shoved into the alleyway at the bottom of Prospect Terrace where they were brutally beaten up; arms and legs were broken, faces slashed, blood everywhere and when it was thought that they had been taught a lesson the defenders of Sidmouth Street disappeared from the scene.

This little fracas took place on Saturday afternoon and on Monday it was front-page news in the national dailies, blazed in big, forbidding, block capitals: 'KING'S CROSS GANG'S RIOUTOUS BEHAVIOUR', 'INNOCENT CITIZENS ATTACKED', 'LONDON GANGS MARAUD THE STREETS', 'INNOCENT PEDESTRIANS ASSAULTED IN SIDMOUTH STREET'. They were full of it, and there was nothing about poor old Solly's window being smashed. Police from another area came banging on doors in an attempt to identify the culprits but it was futile.

The press kept the pressure up for the rest of the week. I think another of Mosley's mobs took a similar battering elsewhere. Roscoe and his little army maintained their vigilance, expecting a revenge attack at any minute, but the Blackshirts kept away from our part of the Gray's Inn Road and never bothered the area again. They tried to get a meeting going in Chapel Street in Somers Town but yet again they received a hiding.

30

Helping Out Abe

Towards the end of 1936 I packed in the job with Pickford's. About the same time I enrolled in an evening class at St Martin's School of Art so that I could continue with my music lessons. This was partly because my mother pleaded with me not to waste what she believed was my vocation in life. She really believed that my destiny lay in music. Mum had a point: so by enrolling I at least made her happy.

St Martin's had its premises in one of the more unsavoury areas of the West End of London. Outside the gates of this highly-thought-of school were Pulteney and Berwick Street markets, and just to the east were the vice dens of Soho. In our small class of seven pupils there were four of us on violin, a couple of girls struggling to learn the cello and one on guitar. The class would start at seven thirty sharp, with each of us giving a rendering of whatever practice pieces we had been given the week before. The tutors were usually members of the bigger London orchestras and it was their way of earning a bit on the side. Everything was very easy-going but we learnt something about music and how it was constructed. And so I met up with Ron who, like me, was doing a stint at St Martin's to please his parents. We both enjoyed making music but got mightily bored with the technical side. We were both young and all we wanted to do was to copy our favourites. Like me and my other pals, Ron and I couldn't get enough of Django Reinhardt and Stéphane Grappelli, much to the annoyance of our tutor who looked on any form of modern music as an abomination.

Ron's family had come to England to escape some sort of oppression in Italy. His real name was Ronaldo. The family name was Beretta but they called themselves Barrett and owned a small restaurant just around the corner from Percy Street, to the west of the Tottenham Court Road. After class at St Martin's, Ron and I usually spent an hour or two there, supping coffee and munching the occasional sandwich, all supplied free of charge. Ron's Mum and Dad seemed happy that their son had a mate who shared his interest in music. Ron was far more gifted than I would ever be, but we worked well together and when we played as a duo in the restaurant the customers seemed to enjoy our efforts, even if we weren't quite up to the standard of Grappelli and Reinhardt. The infamous Fitzroy Tavern was just around the corner from Percy Street and if the Tavern's clientele needed a cup of decent coffee to sober them up after a day's carousing it was to Ron's family restaurant that they wended their unsteady way. So the place was always full with a ragbag of writers, poets and other arty-crafty hangabouts. I had drawn my last pay packet from Pickford's on the Friday and, the following Wednesday, Ron and I were sitting in the restaurant enjoying a cup of tea and I was moaning about finding worthwhile work when up to our table comes a big, burly character. 'You out of a job, son?' I must have nodded or said something to the affirmative. 'I can give you a job if you're not too particular,' says this bloke. 'You won't make a fortune but it's work and if you do a good job, you'll get well paid. Can you ride a bike?'

'Can a duck swim? Of course I can ride a bike.' The man handed me two one pound notes. 'That will see you through to next Monday.' Then he gave me an address in Denmark Street. 'Be there at nine on Monday and we'll have a chat', and with that he was up and away. 'Do you know who he is?' I asked Ron. 'I don't know him except he's one of our regulars.' That was it then. I'd got money in my pocket and a job to start the following week. My worries were over. Then somebody shouted, 'Come on, you two kids, give us a tune.' Ron and I obliged with 'Honeysuckle Rose'. When we'd finished all and sundry gave us a good clap but nobody thought of passing the hat round, so we broke all the rules by giving our services for free.

On Monday morning I walked round to a ground-floor-shop-cum-office in Denmark Street. I'd found out the man's name was Abe Marks. He told me he made his money running errands for local businesses. 'I'll get a call and you go round and deliver what's wanted. Remember, we guarantee speed, we're the quickest postal service in the city. The most important part of this job is that you deliver to the person named and no one else. Do the job, don't poke yer nose in what don't concern yer, and you get fifty bob a week. Usually five days a week but you never know when you may be needed, the bike's out the back, and Mrs Barnes comes in twice a week to sort things out. She's nothing to do with you.'

I made off out the back to find a fairly new bike with a small front wheel to allow for the long box that was fixed to the front of the machine. I pumped the tyres up board-hard, trimmed the brakes, adjusted the saddle and then I was ready to start earning my fifty bob, an enormous wage for a lad not yet seventeen.

At first I spent my time charging round central London delivering small parcels, mail that couldn't wait for the morrow, rolls of blueprints and plans to building sites, that sort of thing. I was doing everything that the couriers who dash round London today on motorcycles do, but I was years ahead of my time. Abe gave me my orders for the day and then he'd say: 'I'll be off then, son. Got some business to settle. If I'm not back when you're finished you can buzz off home.' The job was that cushy.

Of all the people I have worked for Abe Marks was the most colourful. His normal dress was a shabby pair of nonde-script trousers held up by a pair of extra-wide braces and a belt that slipped down below his sagging belly. He always wore a bow tie: perhaps he thought it was in keeping with the bohemian lifestyle of Soho. On his feet he usually wore a pair of worn-out carpet slippers. He only dressed a bit more smartly when he had to go and visit one of his clients. He didn't normally wear a hat and his bald patch made him look like an egg. He had a perpetual grin which seemed to cut his face in half. Abe was a character with a capital C.

I never discovered why my predecessor had left Abe's employment, but after a bit I realised that working for Abe carried a certain amount of risk.

I had discovered that one of Abe's most profitable sidelines was getting rid of stolen property that the usual fences wouldn't touch. This sort of stolen stuff was taken round to Abe who passed it to me, making sure that he never actually touched it so there were no fingerprints on it. Then he would say, 'Take this little lot round to Connie in Kirby Street.' Kirby Street ran parallel to Hatton Garden and Farringdon Road. Connie the jeweller would melt down the gold, reshape the stones and sell the results in Hatton Garden. I then went and got the cash, and after everybody had had their cut, including the nutters who had stolen the stuff in the first place, Abe would pocket the rest. There were gangs involved and if you upset them they could play it rough.

Once on one of these errands, loaded with incriminating evidence, I biked out of Hatton Garden, and in my usual mad manner belted along St Cross Street and crashed into a car parked on the corner of Kirby Street. The driver wound down his window and shouted, 'You'll kill yerself going around like that, sonny boy.' As soon as I heard the words 'sonny boy' I realised that it was the law sitting in the car so I didn't do the drop but went straight back to Abe. 'OK, Vic, do it later, they won't sit there all day.' Abe was right.

The week after I started with Abe Marks, Ron suggested that maybe we could earn ourselves a bit of pocket money by playing the theatre queues. I immediately agreed and off we went. We played the usual Grappelli stuff that we knew so well and at first things went quite smoothly until one day outside the Lyric Theatre on Shaftesbury Avenue we were accosted by a couple of smart-looking men who wanted to know who we thought we were working pitches without permission. One of them was twisting a knuckle-duster around his hand. Ron didn't seem to understand the drill, but I knew. 'Come on, Ron, it's time to scarper. Sorry, mate,' I said to one of the heavies, 'we didn't know.' And so ended our brief excursion into the kerbside entertainment business.

About five or six weeks later Abe called me in from the backyard where I was doing something to the bike. 'Got a special for you today, Vic. Remember what I told you when you first came, deliver to who you're told and no one else, if the person isn't there then bring the package back, got it?' I nodded. 'Good.' He told me to go to a café in Windmill Street (just off the Dilly). 'Ask for Sid. He'll give you a package and an address, you've got fifteen minutes to get to the café, don't forget, no one but . . .' With that I was sent on my way.

Sid was chewing on a fag waiting outside the café when I arrived. 'Know what you got to do, son?' 'Yep, good as done,' I answered. 'Cheeky sod, ain't yer?' said Sid. I was to meet this man who would be waiting outside the Dominion Cinema at St Giles Circus. 'He's a big bloke, short back and sides, wiv a brown coat. Can't be missed, just call him uncle.'

I met up with the man Sid had described and handed over the dosh. I had no doubt that there were pound notes in the package. He gave a grunt and then he was on his way. I took one look at his shoes: I could tell a copper in a blackout. When I got back to Denmark Street, Abe asked if everything had gone OK. 'No problems.' I was beginning to have my doubts about Abe. He was a real fixer, no question. Forget the cover, the letters and suchlike, Abe's true role in life was fencing stolen property for the local villains and organising the payment of dropsy to those in power who could do the arresting, in other words the police.

A new gang was now beginning to make its presence felt in the manor. The Yiddishers, as they were called, were already established in the East End, Bethnal Green, Shoreditch and the like, and had risen to prominence because of their hostility to Mosley's Blackshirts. I was certain that Roscoe had asked for their support in our little do in Sidmouth Street. If I was right, it meant that Roscoe was obliged to them and was expected to return the favour, if and when asked, no matter what – that's the way things worked.

To top it off, I realised that Abe was heavily involved with one of the most vicious mobs of the time, the Elephant Boys, a gang who wielded a big stick on the streets of south London. Abe carried on touting his wares without a care in the world. When I mentioned this to Roscoe he just shrugged. 'Silly sod's supposed to know it all, ain't 'e? 'E's some sort of go-between, is 'e? A fixer like you said, Vic? Bound to get nobbled or cut. If I were you I'd scarper out of it. Forget about the dosh, you can always fiddle a bob or two.' That was Roscoe's reasoning and I couldn't have agreed more. Getting a fistful of dosh for doing some character 'a good turn' was one thing; getting a cutthroat razor flashing about in front of your face was a different kettle of fish.

I thought maybe I'd stay for a few more weeks, see what happened.

One day Abe called me into the little cubby-hole he called his office; broom cupboard more like. He had a telephone fixed up and a couple of writing pads and pinned to the walls he had two huge maps of central London and the docks down by Silvertown. He pulled out a stool from under the table. 'Got a special little job I want yer to 'elp me out wiv.'

31

A Bit of Prestige

What Abe was trying to tell me, while at the same time not giving too much away, was that the Sabinis were trying to enlist the help of the Hoxton Boys and the Yiddishers in an alliance against the common enemy, the Elephant Boys. These were some of the strongest gangs in London.

The Elephant Boys came from the other side of the river, somewhere west of the Elephant and Castle, and were the biggest name in the south. The Sabinis approached Abe to see if he could set up a meeting. These rival gangs hated each other. The whole of Soho knew that the Elephant Boys were testing the water and as a preliminary had set up a group of girls to work along the Oxford Street end of Greek Street, right on the Hoxton Boys' patch. By this time Abe knew that I had sussed out his wheeling and dealing and as I was now delivering the handouts to half of West End Central – the Savile Row cops, that is – he must have felt that I was to be trusted. In my mates' eyes I was now acquiring prestige, but the danger of this notoriety was that if Abe overstepped the mark, and it was thought that he wasn't showing due respect, he would get done over and probably me with him. For all his cunning it seemed to me that he was completely unaware of the danger. These gangs had no qualms whatever about inflicting injury on their enemies. They were experts in the use of cutthroat razors and would use these fearful instruments at the slightest provocation.

I was by now so sure of my ability to keep out of real trouble that, in spite of the difference in our ages, I never felt overawed by Abe. When he had finished telling me everything, I said: 'Abe, don't tell me any more. I was raised with the Hoxton Boys, I know all about the Sabinis, and what I've heard about this Elephant mob is enough to give anyone nightmares for life. Don't even consider me taking any part in whatever escapade you're planning. Leave me out, I'll work until the end of the week then I'm off. If you've got your head screwed on properly then you'll give up any idea of working with that lot. If you work for one of them you'll become an enemy of the others. You'll finish up being cut up at the very least.' Then Abe said, 'What you mean by saying you used to work wiv the Hoxton lot?' 'As a kid, I used to run errands for them, I know all about them. I tumbled what you're up to in the first three weeks. What you're thinking about, Abe, is dodgy, lay off it.' I added: 'Another thing, Abe, you're a Jewboy, you should understand that the Yiddishers will never get into a deal wiv the Hoxton lot seeing that the Hoxton lot are all in sympathy wiv Mosley. Fink about it, Abe.'

So the best paying boss I ever had slipped into history, too. About six weeks after I finished with Abe, I was in the restaurant with Ron and I happened to ask him if Abe still came in. 'You mean the Jewboy you was working for?' 'Yeh.' 'We heard he got picked up. 'E's doing three months in Wandsworth, aiding and abetting, no big deal.'

I found time to go round to the West End nick where I learnt that Abe had indeed come to their notice and, yes, it was true, he was doing three months in Wandsworth. I wanted to see him so I went to the prison to arrange a date. I got a collection up for him and bought some fags and baccy, along with a few other goodies. It was really great to see the look of happiness and joy when he was marched in and spotted me with the goodies. 'You're the only visitor I've had,' said Abe. 'You're some smart kid. I should have listened.' It appeared that in deciding that he was indeed treading 'in deep shit' he had told the Hoxton Boys that he wanted out and the gang's answer was to stitch him up. They gave Abe a nice little earner of a dodgy job and then let out a word to one of their contacts at Savile Row nick. In a wink Abe was picked up with the incriminating goods, charged and sent down. To the Hoxton Boys' way of thinking no harm had been done to Abe; they'd just given him a gentle reminder that in future when they said jump, he jumped. I don't think Abe took it all that hard. When he came out he continued doing the deliveries and such, kept everybody happy, earned nice money but he had learnt his lesson: always know your place.

Things were looking up for our little family. Working for Abe, I'd been able to give our mum another thirty bob a week, Brother John was still working his way into the high-class grocery business, sister Emmy was coming up for eleven and our mum was getting worried about the boys she was knocking around with. To cap it all the Ministry of Defence, or whatever they were called then, was ordering hats by the thousands and all the milliners and hat-makers were hard at it to fill the sudden demand. Mum was earning a bomb, but she earned it the hard way, even bringing home work to finish off in the evening. Granddad got tired of hearing Mum's old treadle sewing machine thumping away so he bought her an electric motor and our Uncle Frank, who was clever at that sort of thing, fixed it to the Singer. So things could have been worse, but I had to find some more gainful employment.

32

Horror Job

My next job was so bad that even writing about it makes me want to throw up. Via the employment exchange, I was hired as an apprentice machine minder in a small factory. I was told that in a couple of years, when I finished the apprenticeship, I would be earning wages beyond my wildest dreams. The price I had to pay was that for the next two years I had to work for rock-bottom money. I even had to sign a form agreeing that I was bound to the firm for a period of not less than twenty-four months. My mum and granddad were very pleased. 'Good, learn a trade, set you up for life.' By the time of my seventeenth birthday in October I had had enough of the steady job. If I remember, it was around midweek. I just switched off the lathe, went up to the office and told them that I would be absent from now on, or words to that effect. The foreman came in and demanded that I get back to work. I just walked out of the door and that was that.

Next morning I realised that they still had my cards and that I had signed on for two years. What I hadn't reckoned on was the attitude of the labour exchange in Penton Street. When I went up to sign on I was told in no uncertain terms that I had put myself out of work. Result: no dole, find another job on your own, you get no money from us.

I'd show 'em. Get another job? Simple: I'd done it before, I could do it again.

Part Three

33

Covent Garden and Maisie

About a week later, skint and without a penny to my name, I was standing on the corner of Long Acre and Endell Street at nine in the morning taking in the hustle and bustle of Covent Garden Market. With all the noise, the shouts of the shopkeepers hiring the barrow boys to collect the produce from the general dealers and cart it round to the stalls in the market for them, it was bedlam. Then I spotted a bloke struggling on his own, shifting sacks of potatoes from the outside of his shop to stack them up inside. I walked over. 'Need any 'elp, mister?'

'Course 'e needs 'elp.'

The voice that answered my enquiry came from a woman about the same age as the bloke. The man stopped what he was doing and gave me the once-over. 'Can yer lift these sacks of spuds?' I heaved one on to my shoulder. 'Where yer want it?' Before the man could answer the woman interrupted. She gave me my orders as if we had been lifelong friends. 'Everything outside has to come in, keep the piles separate, the tats by that wall, the soft fruit over there. Anything that's going rotten you sweep into the gutter.' I looked at the man I had offered to help. 'That's the wife, son,' he said, 'she's the boss, if you can do it then get cracking.' The woman was seated at a large roll-top desk in the corner of the shop, lit by a 160-watt bulb under a huge enamel shade that hung about a foot above her head. By her side there was an old, round Valor oil stove which she would occasionally put her hands over to keep her fingers warm. It was the only warm spot in the entire shop. Her name was Maisie and her old man was called Sammy.

Maisie was always on the phone, which never stopped ringing. With the phone in one hand and a pencil in the other, she wrote the orders down on a piece of paper and then impaled them on a long spike embedded in the wall by her side. As soon as Sammy had got the orders ready from the last lot of phone calls he would grab a handful of new orders from the spike. It was non-stop stuff. At least it kept us warm. There was no way that either me or Sammy would feel the cold while we were going at this speed.

I set to with a will and inside ten minutes I was aching in parts of my body that I didn't know existed. 'Take a blow, son, the world ain't gonna end today.' By the time all the goods were stacked inside the shop it was getting on for eleven. 'Sammy, you go round and have yer breakfast and put the boy's name on the slate. We'll finish clearing up.' 'Wot's yer name, son?' I told her. 'Don't forget, Sammy, 'is name is Victor.' Sammy took off his apron, put on a scruffy jacket and disappeared into the crowd outside.

'What we do now, Victor, is sweep the pavement, lock up the shutters and that's it until tomorrow.' I couldn't believe it. 'What, you mean you're finished for the day?' 'Of course,' said Maisie, 'but we've been here since three this morning, that's when the really 'ard work starts. When Sammy gets back you go round to Bernie's in Floral Street and have a good breakfast. Don't worry, it's paid for, fill yer plate up, you've earned it, and after that come back 'ere and we'll all 'ave a little natter. That's if you're interested in a job.' With that she threw a big heavy broom at me and pointed to the door. 'The pavement, Vicky boy.'

When Sammy returned he sent me off to Bernie's, which turned out to be a typical market café: all the windows steamed up from the inside, an overpowering aroma of steamed and boiled food combined with the smell of a thousand fags, pipes and small cigars, plus the clatter of plates and cutlery and the non-stop chatter that was part and parcel of any working men's café.

'Sammy sent me round,' I said to the woman behind the counter. 'Leaving it a bit late, ain't yer?' she replied. ''E only just sent me round.' 'What is it then, breakfast?' 'Yes please, missus.' 'I like the "please",' she quips back. 'Don't ofen 'ear that in 'ere.' Up came a huge plate with enough food to feed an army. It was all there: two eggs, bacon, black pudding, tomatoes and a couple of doorsteps of bread, fried almost black – the whole lot emptied out of a seemingly yard-wide frying pan. I found a seat and was tucking in when she came over with the biggest mug of steaming hot tea I had ever seen. 'Fergot yer tea,' she said.

After I had gulped the whole lot down and nearly recovered from heaving the heavy sacks about, I staggered back to the shop. The shutters were up and locked, and Sammy and his wife were sitting inside drinking a cup of tea. 'That's it then,' said Sammy, 'another day done.' 'You can turn up tomorrow if you want to,' said Maisie.

I didn't need to think twice. 'Yes please, missus, I would like to.' 'Right,' she says. 'We open up the shutters at as near as dammit three in the morning. You and Sammy 'ave a break at about six, then you get a breakfast about ten, finished for the day by eleven. Today's Wednesday, so we will pay you daily until next week and if you're still with us at the end of the week you can start regular like, two pounds ten shillings a week. We pay for your breakfast and you can take all the veg your mum needs, providing yer don't get greedy. I'll pay yer twelve shilling a day until Saturday. And it can be bloody cold at three in the morning, Victor. 'Ave you got a better pair of boots than those you've got on now?' 'No, I ain't,' I said. 'Well, we'll see what we've got at 'ome. Don't come in after three thirty, get orf 'ome wiv yer now and get some kip.' And that was it. I'd got another job.

Maisie was dead right. I staggered off home, dropped on my bed and conked out. Mum woke me up when she came home from work. 'What's the matter, Victor, you feeling ill, like?' 'No, Mum, just knackered.' I told her about the new job. 'You'll be the death of me, Victor,' she said. 'How on earth are you going to get up at two in the morning?' Mum had hit the nail on the head. Three o'clock hadn't sounded so bad, but I hadn't reckoned on the time I would have to get up in order to get to the Garden by three. 'Is it a good job then?' she asked. 'Best yet,' I said and told her about my morning's experiences. 'The lady who runs the shop says these clothes ain't no good for the job but I fink she's going to sort somefink out. You know what, Mum, I think they need someone to 'elp them out, I don't think that this bloke Sammy is in the best of 'ealth.' 'Well, get to bed by nine at the latest. I'll see what I can rake up to keep you warm and we can borrow Granddad's alarm clock until you get your own.' Mum disappeared downstairs to break the news to my grand-dad and grandmother. I had no doubt that I was in their bad books yet again. 'Didn't give 'im the strap enough when 'e was young, no discipline, think they can come and go as they like.' All the usual stuff. I'd show 'em.

Grandfather's alarm clock was a real contraption, a huge clockface with two bell-like things on either side and a sort of clapper that hit the bells when the alarm went off. Enough noise to wake the dead. It could have woken up half of Holborn. When it did go off, could I find the button to switch it off? Neither me nor my mum had given that little matter any thought, so I shoved it into my bed to try and smother the noise.

By the time it had stopped I had given myself a lick with freezing cold tap water, Mum had cooked a bacon sandwich and I was pedalling as fast as I could, steering the bike with one hand and finishing off the remains of the bacon sand-wich with the other. I arrived in Long Acre as the church clock chimed 2.30. Mum had put the alarm clock on half an hour: 'Just in case.' But, even so, the whole area was alive

– shutters were being opened, chains being taken away from the lines of sack trucks and barrows, some men were having their last lounge about and a fag before the real work of the morning began.

The first part of the day had already happened with the arrival from the railway stations of the carts that delivered the hundreds of different sorts of vegetables to the big wholesalers who were based in the market itself. Just before the church clock struck three, a horse and cart drew up outside the place of my new employers, and down jumped Sammy and Maisie, while the driver of the cart tethered the horse to the lamp post outside the shop. Maisie gave me a hug. 'You made it then, Victor, bit cold in them clothes, 'ain't yer?' 'Ow long yer been 'ere then?' Sammy chimed in, and he also seemed glad that I had turned up. I told him. 'Come on then, Victor, let's get the shutters down and then Maisie will 'ave a nice cuppa ready. By the way, this is Maisie's bruvver Bert. You won't see much of 'im except when we unload the goods.' Bruvver Bert looked older than his sister. It turned out that it was Bert who did all the buying from the big wholesalers. The goods were stacked up in bushel and hundredweight sacks. A shouter yelled out the price of the commodities, up went the hands and a call was made for whatever quantity was desired. Once the deal was done the market porters carted it around to the premises of the buyer. There was no haggling about how much the porters were paid; there were unwritten laws about all of that. Maisie looked after the booking side of the deliveries, Sammy, and now me, stacked the orders on to the cart. While we were doing this, Bert disappeared round the corner to Bernie's where, with the other carters, he tucked into one of their enormous breakfasts.

'Vicky boy,' says Sammy, 'yer got to learn to stack the cart in the proper manner. Bert's got to be able to get at the order when he gets to the customer.' Sammy let me into the mysteries of loading a horse-drawn cart. As for the horse itself, it was a huge beast, contentedly eating away at whatever was stashed inside the nosebag that was permanently fixed to its head. In the gutter there was evidence of the gallons of water the beast had supped up en route from Stepney to Long Acre. Bert came back from Bernie's, Maisie gave him his orders and off he trotted.

Bert delivered to some of the biggest hotels in the district, anywhere that had a large restaurant. With Bert gone, Sammy and me prepared the orders for the customers with smaller establishments who turned up with their own form of transport. By now it was eight o'clock – what with loading the cart and the comings and goings of the other customers the time had passed in a flash.

Maisie sold only the best. Any item of vegetable that was deemed not up to standard was thrown on the waste pile, and by the amount of rubbish that was collecting along the side of the road it seemed that this is what was done by the market in general.

By nine thirty things began to slow down a bit. 'I'm off, then,' says Sammy to his missus and he disappeared around to Bernie's.

I sat down on a sack of spuds and Maisie came over. 'Yer done well, Victor, we're all pleased wiv yer. Now look 'ere,

I've brought some of Sammy's bruvver's clothes, if yer want 'em. 'Is bruvver died a couple of weeks ago, that's why we were short'anded.' She produced an old potato sack with a pair of heavy boots, a couple of pairs of thick twill trousers, a thick shirt, a leather apron and a big iron hook. 'We wasn't going to give 'em to yer until Monday,' said Maisie, 'but if yer keep at it like you bin, then you can consider it that you're well in. Don't worry, all the gear 'as bin washed and scrubbed. Seeing it's not far out of our way we'll give yer a lift 'ome on the cart. Now, as soon as Bert gits back you go an' eat.'

I was dumbfounded. 'I'll tell yer what, missus,' I said. 'I'm not very good at keeping jobs, but I promise to do my best.' I'd never spoken to anyone in that way before. It was like I was talking to my mum. Then Maisie said: 'And between you and me, Victor, Sammy ain't too well neither. If yer see 'im struggling, barge in and give 'im an' 'and, and fer gawd's sake stop calling me missus. My name is Maisie and proud of it.'

After I had returned from the café, Sammy gave me instructions on how best to use the hook. 'Just stick it in the sack and 'eave,' he said, 'much easier than tearing yer fingers to bits, don't take the 'ook 'ome, if the law catches you wiv it it's an offensive weapon.' I could well believe it. What a weapon: stick it in anyone's head and you're on a dangler (the end of a rope).

Bert returned to the fold having finished his part of the day's work. I put the bike on to the tailboard of the cart and off we trundled, up Drury Lane along Broad Street into Kingsway, Russell Square and home. 'Bit of a posh neighbourhood this, ain't it, Victor?' said Maisie. No one had ever called it posh before.

Maisie was right about the clothes. My mum didn't have to alter anything: even the boots fitted. 'They seem to be good people,' said Mum as she surveyed the clothing and the fresh veg I had brought home. ''Ard work, is it?' 'Very 'ard, Mum, but the time goes quick.'

So now I was hard at it, dressed like a market man, slaving like a market man and knackered when I'd finished for the day. I had never grafted as hard as this, but it was certainly toning me up, and all the while I was learning a completely new way of life.

I found out that all the market traders were family enter-prises, almost all of them come from areas east of Aldwych – Stepney, Shoreditch, Whitechapel, Bethnal Green and the like. Some of them could trace their history at the Garden back two hundred years. The porters were the top dogs. These men, when not pushing a barrow piled up with veg, put the stuff in round baskets piled up on their heads; they could carry as many as ten baskets at a time. I was a gentile in the middle of a crowd of Yiddishers. There was no friction; the whole system worked like a well-oiled machine. With every day that I worked, the more I enjoyed myself. As well as which, I was putting on weight and growing stronger. Maisie was delighted when, one morning, we had to open up and the rain was coming down by the bucketful. 'We'll 'ave to pull the blinds down,' said Sammy. I'd often wondered about these blinds. The other shops pulled them down at the slightest excuse but this was the first time they had been mentioned in the three weeks I'd been there. Sammy got a long pole with a massive metal hook on the end. 'It takes three of us to pull them down,' said Sammy, at which I hooked the pole into the slot in the blinds and with a hard pull down came the whole long blind which covered the entire front of the shop. 'Bloody hell,' said Sammy. 'What you been putting in your porridge?' It was a really great feeling getting praised for doing those blinds. I could feel my muscles rippling under the weight of adulation.

34

Boxing Clubs and the Palais de Danse

For a year, Roscoe, a couple of his mates and me had been members of a sporting club in Islington which specialised in boxing. One of Roscoe's pals, a chap who went by the good old east London name of Ruby Bernstein, had a brother who worked in Jack Solomon's office in Great Windmill Street. Jack was the number one promoter of the day, and if by chance you passed by the 'shop', as it used to be called, you could see groups of hopefuls waiting to be introduced to the great man himself, and with a bit of luck get on to a programme as a filler, the small six-rounder fights that kept the punters amused before the main event.

Ruby's brother could be relied on to get tickets for any decent fight we wanted to see, usually at the local baths, sometimes up the Cally, sometimes in Hoxton. He could even wangle seats for the Ring at Blackfriars, which, after the Harringey Arena and the Royal Albert Hall, was the main fight arena in London. We loved everything about boxing. Of all the clubs to be found in the back alleys of working-class areas, it was the boxing clubs that attracted the young boys the most. Here was a way of climbing out of the dirt and grime and into the big time. All you had to do was to get in the ring and destroy anyone who stood in your path to fame and glory. Young men would pummel away at each other trying to get noticed and get on a programme. They got knocked down, got hurt, came up for more – and each one kidded himself that he was the best.

So the four of us used to spend our evenings up in Islington watching the young hopefuls sparring with each other. One evening, the four of us were in a corner of the gym, supping bottles of almost non-alcoholic light ale, when one of the trainers sat down among us and asked, 'When are we going to see which of you lot is any good? When are you going to get in the ring and 'ave a dust-up, you've bin comin' 'ere long enough, we ain't yet seen what you're capable of?'

Well, none of us four were going to start walloping each other, so Roscoe ups and suggests that he find someone about eleven stone, and 'Vic will sort 'im out'. The trainer gives me the eye. 'OK wiv you then, mate?' 'Sure,' says I, feeling my new-found strength. In no time at all the chairs are gathered around the ring and I'm beginning to have second thoughts as I make my way to the dressing room where I'm kitted out with a singlet and a pair of gloves. In the meantime the trainer has produced the lad he wanted to get the fight for in the first place. He weighed in at just under twelve stone; I was giving away about ten pounds plus my complete inexperience. I wasn't too bothered by what I was giving away, and I was bolstered by the shouts of my gang of supporters. I had no doubt that the hulk having his gloves tied up would soon be sitting on the floor wondering what had hit him.

They didn't have a proper bell so one of the club sidekicks bashed two plates together and we went at it hammer and tongs. I managed the first, second and third rounds with only a small amount of blood coming from my nose. Between the rounds Ruby fanned me with a scruffy bit of towel, telling me that this bloke ain't going to last another round, ''E's 'ad it, Vic. One good wallop and it's all over.'

Out we came for the fourth go at each other. I was feeling pretty pleased with myself when the stupid sod in front of me led with his left as if to give me a cruncher in the gut, and as I went down to cover he brought over a right that connected with the middle of my face. Back I went under the impact, back and back until I was sliding down below the ropes. I thought I'd been hit by a bulldozer. I could dimly hear Roscoe and his mates yelling for me to get up and 'kill the sod'. When I finally tottered to my feet the bloke refereeing had sent the other lad back to his seat and declared me dead, game over sort of thing. Then the lad who'd been responsible for the damage to my face came over and asked me if I was OK. 'Yep, I'm OK, see you another time,' I says. 'Not before you learn to keep yer guard up,' he says.

'You don't 'arf look a bit ropey', said Roscoe on the tram back. 'Thanks to you lot,' I said, and they laughed all the way home. When I turned up for work on the Monday morning and they all asked how I got my face done up, I had to endure another bout of hilarity. 'Who was yer fighting, wasn't Kid Berg was it?' The only one who didn't see the funny side of all this was Maisie. 'I bet yer mum told yer orf then, that's all you men think about, sex and fighting.' I was in her bad books for a few hours but by the end of the day she had relented. 'You won't get anywhere by fighting, Victor.' It was as if I was listening to Mum.

After that I was determined to learn to keep my guard up, not because I was interested in boxing as a career, but just in case I ran across the hulk who had tried to alter the shape of my face. As it happened I had the last laugh. Roscoe got hold of a couple of tickets to the Royal Albert Hall for a battle royal between his idol, Harry Mizler, who was having another go at defeating Jimmy Walsh. This was early in 1937. Harry won the fight and, as we were celebrating, a gang of Jimmy's supporters started wading into us. Roscoe came away from that little fracas with his big Jewish conk bent almost backwards, from which it never seemed to recover.

I was now working in the market as though I had done so all my life. To Maisie's delight Sammy was doing all the light work while all the heavy lifting fell on my shoulders, which were getting broader by the day.

One morning when we were alone, Maisie said: 'You know, Victor, I'm real pleased that you've taken all the 'ard work off of Sammy, but you got to be gentle about it. If he starts thinking that 'e carn't pull 'is weight any more it will effect 'im. Let 'im do a bit now and again but, like yer doing now, keep an eye on 'im.' And then, as if on impulse, she bent over and planted a kiss on my forehead.

'Sorry about that, Victor, but the good Lord never saw fit to bless us wiv a little one and you're the only one we've met that would fit the bill.' After a slight pause and a little wipe of her eyes, 'There, Victor, I've only said what the pair of us have been thinking, perhaps I've upset you?' 'No, you 'avn't done that, missus, I was thinking all along that Sammy would 'ave made a nice dad.' Whereupon Maisie burst into a flood of tears.

Later that year, some time in May, Sammy dropped to the floor while we were loading up Bert's cart. In no time the ambulance arrived and Sammy was on his way to Charing Cross Hospital. Maisie wanted him to stay off work for at least a week after he got out, but as soon as Sammy could get out of bed he was back on the job and Maisie's face was lined with anxiety. By now I was earning the enormous wage of three pounds a week, almost as much as my granddad. Maisie and Bert didn't want me to leave; as it was they were just hanging on by the skin of their teeth.

The days were getting warmer and Sammy's health improved although, when we were in the shop by ourselves, Maisie kept on about not letting Sammy do too much. 'Let 'im think 'e's doing it, Victor, but I'm relying on you to make sure he don't do too much.' 'Don't worry, Mum.' I'd started calling Maisie 'Mum'. I don't know why; it just seemed to be the right expression, and she never challenged me about it.

By now Maisie knew all about my life. During the slack periods she used to ask me about my family: what it was like living in Holborn, what school I had gone to and so on. I told her everything – about my dad leaving home, the months I'd spent in the Shaftesbury Home, about my mates and the way we all stuck together, being frightened of no one. I told her how I wanted to make my fortune and how I liked working for her and Sammy. She said, 'You don't need to make a fortune, Victor, all you have to do is to play it straight with those around you, never tell lies and, if you do wrong, face up to it and admit it. Live like that and you will have a happy life, maybe not rich, but happy.'

She said that, despite the misfortune with my dad, my mum was lucky to have not one but three lovely children. When Maisie let herself go like this, as she did on several occasions, it always ended in tears which she tried to hide, but couldn't.

Was there any difference between our mum and Maisie? I think there was.

Maisie could command attention. Even the hulking great porters buckled when she had a go at them for not doing things as she saw wanted doing. Mum could never have been as forceful as that, but, if it came down to what was right and what was wrong, they were as alike as two peas in a pod.

I told Maisie about Peggy, how we had been born and bred in the same streets and how she fancied me and how she had gone off with this stupid ginger-haired sod who I was sure was going to start beating her up, and when that happened I would have to go charging in and rescue her. I could never have told my mum these things. Maisie sat in her chair by the desk, with her hands over the old Valor heater, and listened silently until, at some break in my meanderings, she would try to sort things out for me. 'You have to understand, Victor, that a woman has different feelings to a man.'

Then she would go on and on, just like my mum and gran. What is it about women? Sometimes after these sessions with Maisie I used to ride my bike round to the street where Peggy lived. I didn't see her so I rode round again hoping that if we did bump into each other we could have a chat, just to see how things are going. I'd make certain she was OK and not being beaten by the ginger-haired sod. But we never did meet. Maisie once told me that I would probably miss Peggy all my life because she was my first love, and, 'Man or woman, it makes no difference, we're all the same. You never forget that first introduction to the great mystery of life.'

Back in the market the talk was all about what was going on in Germany. Meetings were held on street corners which the police tried to break up. I think that was because there was such a large Jewish community in the market: they were more aware of the danger of what might happen if Hitler was allowed to carry on unrestrained.

I was coming home after an enjoyable evening playing in the café with Ron, which we now did on a regular basis (my music gear was a permanent fixture in Ron's bedroom), when I bumped into Roscoe and two of his mates. I didn't know them but if they were mates of Roscoe they must have been OK. We all agreed that a fistful of fish and chips was a good idea, so off we headed to the fish shop in Kenton Street.

We arrived to find the place surrounded by the local fuzz who were loading half a dozen screaming girls into a Black Maria. We learnt that three new girls had tried to operate on the patch of three of the regulars who, naturally, took offence and started a fight.

Roscoe's mate Billy sussed it all out in a flash. 'Someone's trying to muscle in, some gang probably. Who's running this lot 'ere?' I wasn't certain but guessed it must be the Somers Town lot. 'That's Charlie Donahue,' pipes up Dusty, Roscoe's other mate, who lived in Ossulton Street, right next to Somers Town goods station. We all knew that this meant trouble we'd be better off out of. The problem was we all lived in the vicinity, and I lived right opposite the girls' patch and was known as a wide boy. Not that I personally took part in criminal activities, but I did associate with the lads whose big brothers were running the gangs. They were into protection rackets, burglary and, of course, prostitution, which is where these girls came into the picture. Roscoe and I and his two mates knew all the characters involved, and, more importantly, they knew us.

The following Saturday, Roscoe was sitting in the usual café in Gray's Inn Road, along with his usual retinue of Al Capone lookalikes, when they were called to order by a couple of smartly dressed cutthroats who suggested they all take a walk to the café in the Caledonian Road so they could have a discussion that might be to everyone's advantage. What wasn't said was that refusal was not an option.

It turned out that Dusty had spread the news around that he had seen the girls being put away. The lot who controlled the girls wanted to know more. When Roscoe met them in the other café they asked him who else was involved. Who's this other bloke? Vic? Who's he? What they really wanted to know was who had run the newcomers on to their patch. They were worried that it might turn out to be the Sabinis from Millman Street. Someone chancing their arm could be sorted out with a couple of broken bones, no problem. But if it was the Sabinis that was a different matter. They asked us what we could find out and said to tell the local girls to behave themselves; tell them everything was being 'sorted'.

Afterwards Roscoe dispatched Billy to get me to have a 'meet' with the Somers Town lot to discuss the problems. This was serious stuff. Up to this point we had all steered clear of the courts and now here we were, standing on the brink of, and getting involved in, what could easily turn out to be a vicious gang war.

As far as I was concerned it was nothing to do with us; let them sort out their own troubles. Dusty, who obviously knew a bit more about the mob involved, butted in: 'All very well for you, Vic, but we're with Roscoe and his old man is in a dodgy line of business. You don't think he's doing that without paying his dues? You ought to know the score by now!' I looked across at Roscoe, ''E's right, Vic, we all 'ave to pay our dues. You know the score, works both ways. Nobody interferes wiv our little business, if they ask us to do a favour it's expected we give it the nod.' I still had no idea just what Roscoe's dad did to earn a crust. Then Dusty interrupted: 'Best we go see what they want, ain't no 'arm in that, see what they want and what's in it for us.' We all agreed and left it to Dusty to make the arrangements, after which we shuffled off down the Cross to get a tram up to the Angel and spend the rest of the afternoon in Harry's gym.

Two days later and the four of us are sitting in a café down in Somers Town Market, with some of the heavies from the

Somers Town mob. Dusty knows everyone there, the other three of us are just sitting listening to the chat, and thinking that there's some real hard stuff in here. It was agreed that the Sabinis were trying it on but further proof was needed. They wanted us to get some evidence. Roscoe and Billy gave me a look. I knew what they're thinking: I lived on top of the scene. I piped up that it should be simple: put a tag on the ponce and see where he handed over the dosh. If it was Millman Street then it was the Sabinis. The heavies in the café gave me the hard look. I continued that it was going to cost a few oncers. "Ow much?' 'A fiver should cover it.' One of the gang handed me three one pound notes which he peeled off from a roll done up with an elastic band. We'd get the rest after we'd come up with the goods on the girls. This was their way of telling me that they were in charge and to make sure I knew my place in the scheme of things. I kept my cool and headed for the door, followed by my three mates.

When we were back on familiar territory I told the others not to worry. I told them I'd get a couple of the kids in the street to follow the girls' ponce: we should have results in a couple of days, then that was it, all over, done and dusted. The other three agreed. 'Thought you were going to chicken out, Vic,' said Billy. ''E's not a mate of mine for nuffink,' said Roscoe. Billy didn't know how near the truth he was. I certainly had very nasty feelings about this little job and I knew that finding out who the intruders were would not be the end of it.

I knew enough about the strength of these gangs to understand that, in order to stand up to the Sabinis, the other gangs, who were usually at each other's throats, would have to come together. The other thing was that the only real potential allies with the necessary grunt were the Hoxton lot, and I was the only one of our little gang who was on speaking terms with them, and that was because of my past employer, Abe.

A couple of weeks later we'd supplied the info that it was indeed the Sabinis who were muscling in and they weren't hanging about. A new café had opened on Battle Bridge, the very heart of King's Cross, and it was common knowledge that Sabini money had supplied the down payment, added to which four new girls were operating in Argyle Square, which was a small, quite sedate square considering the neighbourhood that surrounded it. Argyle Square was also the territory of the Islington lot. It was now just over a month since the Sabinis had started extending their territory. The Somers Town lot were going round in circles trying to conjure up enough support to engage the enemy but had made little progress. Then something happened

It was Dusty who came knocking on Roscoe's door. The gang from the Angel had intervened. The ponce who was running the four girls in Argyle Square was now resting in the Royal Free Hospital, just down the road. The girls had been given a warning: 'Don't come back, or else.' The threat was accompanied by a bit of razor waving and the girls were terrified. Having done over the ponce, four of the gang, armed with pick-axe handles, went to the café on Battle Bridge, tied up two Sabini hustlers who happened to be in the café at the time, told the rest of the customers to scarper and then locked the door and started on the café's interior with some gusto. Having satisfied themselves that there was nothing more to smash up, they left.

The whole of the criminal fraternity from King's Cross right up to the Angel held its breath waiting for the next instalment, while the police kept their distance.

What the mob from the Angel had done to the Sabinis and their property, and the fact that there had been no retaliation, did not go unnoticed by the Somers Town lot. The girls in Bernard Street, where the female brawl had kicked it all off, got word to me via the fish and chip shop owner that two of the Sabinis' ponces, 'latinos' as they called them, had been done over and that the invading new girls had gone for good. The Somers Town lot who ran these dozen or so girls in Bernard Street had taken over where the Angel mob had left off and the Sabinis could do nothing about it: not enough troops on the ground to cover their ambitions, that's what it amounted to.

Peace reigned once again.

The Sabinis had one more try to establish their rule on King's Cross turf. They had the café done up again and installed a couple of their seasoned warriors to run it. It didn't work. Roscoe and Billy were approached because it was known that I was with Rozzie and I had access to the Hoxton Mob. The Somers Town mob wanted the Hoxton Boys to force the Sabinis out of the Battle Bridge restaurant so that the whole matter could be sorted out and brought to an end without too much bloodshed.

All I had to do was have a little chat with the Hoxton lads in Dean Street, where they hung out, explain the problem, then pass the answers back to Billy who would pass them on to the bruisers in Somers Town. Roscoe wanted to know if I needed any backup with the Hoxton lot: 'Best on me own, Roz, they don't know you.'

The following afternoon I went to Dean Street, to the den where the Hoxton wide boys hung out. I wasn't worried because I wasn't a threat and I was hoping to meet up with my old cronic Bernie Legget, a Hoxton Mob member who had earned his spurs in gangland by going down for eighteen months even though he was completely innocent. He could have grassed and saved himself but he chose to do the time. By so doing he raised himself up several notches in the esteem of the gang. Bernie was 'in' and Bernie was a mate of mine.

The notorious Hoxton Mob controlled the central London and West End crime scene, protection rackets, prostitution, illegal betting, the lot, as well as which they received dues from a lot of kerbside second-hand car dealers. In return the gang offered immunity from the competition and any other villain who wanted to poach the work. This was the way all the big gangs, including the Sabinis, operated. They also had a lot of the fuzz in their pockets, bunging them nice little – and sometimes not so little – handouts.

The exterior of the small nightclub which the Hoxton boys used as their office was hidden from view by a scruffy builder's hoarding which also hid the steps that led down to the club.

The interior of the club was like all the illegal drinking and gambling dens that had sprung up all over Soho area – dark, plush and smoky. They were very profitable for the gangs that ran them. These gangs always knew if they were going to be raided and when the police arrived all that happened was that a few of the heavies were carted off and given a fine which the gang would pay. That was it: justice done and everyone satisfied.

First it turned out that my old mate Bernie was still residing at His Majesty's pleasure but would be out in a couple of months. I was in trouble: I didn't know anyone there. Then one of the lads looked up from a card school: 'Watcha, Vic, haven't seen you around for a bit.' That's it, I've made contact. The lad who remembered me took me into a small room where a clutch of villains were discussing some future escapade. 'What's your business, mate?' I told them about the girls who were planted in Bernard Street and Argyle Square and about the lads smashing up the Sabinis' restaurant. 'Yeah, but we know all about that caper. What you 'ere for and what's your role in all this?'

I'm starting to feel uneasy but I press on and explain that I'm only the messenger. Tell them that the request is for them to tread on the Sabinis' toes for a couple of weeks while the lads at the Cross and up the Angel sort things out and put paid to the territorial ambitions of the spaghetti eaters. Then one of the gang puts a pint of Whitbread's Best in front of me and I know that the danger is over. While I'm supping up the pint the rest of the group argue the points for and against the proposed alliance.

Eventually they come up with an answer. 'OK, we'll tread on their toes, as you put it, we'll keep them occupied, but the hard stuff is your lot's affair and tell them they're lucky. We know that some of you are in deep with the Yids.' With that ultimatum I knew that I'd done what I'd come for, so it was off as quick as I could out of this den of violence and iniquity. Once up on level ground I took a couple of deep breaths and made my way back to the more civilised world of Ron's café. The gangs would sort it out among themselves. No more bother for us four mates.

One Saturday the four of us decided to visit the new Palais de Danse at Finsbury. Roscoe and Sammy were keen to eye up the latest talent. Billy was starry-eyed over a new piece of skirt he had discovered and said he would have to drag her along with us. None of us wanted our evening spoilt by the tantrums of the other sex but in deference to Billy we agreed she could tag along so long as he kept her under control. Our casual dismissal of the female treasure he now considered to be his property got Billy's juices up but in the end, and muttering to himself, he agreed to 'Keep 'er in 'and'.

So three of us turned up at the Finsbury Park Palais. In no time at all, Roz, who's done up like a prize turkey, is skating around the highly polished floor with the local talent in tow, one at a time, of course. Sammy and me slipped off to the bar where we started supping up and keeping our ears open for the latest news: who's done a handy turn, who's gone down for a session, and, more importantly, what's coming next. The main topic of conversation was the fate of the Sabinis. Billy finally put in an appearance with his bit of skirt and was whisked straight on to the floor before he could so much as say hello to his three mates. Sammy shook his head in despair: 'There yer are, Vic, that's Billy's lot, 'e's 'ad it.' I had to agree.

A year ago there would have been about six, seven or eight of us at these Saturday evening dos; now we were down to four. If this Elsie got her way with poor Billy then we'd be reduced to three. The world was falling apart.

The Finsbury Park Palais de Danse was almost opposite the posh new Astoria Cinema. This area from the Nag's Head to Finsbury Park was outside our manor and was an area noted for its hard nuts. We had no friends in this place and suddenly all hell broke loose. Billy's rolling on the floor having been put there by a bruiser who is defending his girl from an onslaught from Billy's bit of skirt. It turned out that Elsie had objected to the other girl getting a bit too close to her Billy. The home-side girl had retaliated with some help from her friends. We dashed over to help Billy, and as we had no allies to help us it finished up with the four of us getting a real going over from the greater force of the local layabouts. Only Roscoe got away without a scratch. That was the last time we paid a visit to that Palais de Danse. After that, Billy and his girl were thicker than ever.

35

Talking Family

The next bit of trouble to come my way happened when I was woken from my afternoon nap by the sound of my sister Emmy crying. Mum was talking to her in the front room (I was sleeping in the kitchen). I heard Mum ask Emmy: 'Did they do anything to you?' 'They were touching me all over', and then another burst of tears.

'What's happening, Mum?' I asked. 'It's those boys in Herbrand Street, they been messing about with Emmy and her friend.' By this time I've got my coat on and I'm on my way to see if I can round up Roscoe and a couple of our mates. I got to his front door which, as usual, was open to the world, being one of those front doors which was short of a hinge. 'Roscoe, I've got a problem.' I told him the story. 'You know as well as me that if I show my face single-'anded round in Herbrand Street I'm on to a loser. As long as I've got some backing I can sort it out.' 'Gi'us a second, Vic, be right wiv yer. Two of us should be enough, I fink.'

My mate Roscoe looked the business. He never seemed to do any work and yet he'd got the latest gear in overcoats. This one came nearly down to his ankles and the shoulders were padded, making him look much broader than he really was. So we took a short stroll to Herbrand Street. This street was situated less than a hundred yards from Woburn Place; it was on the real outer borders of the devils den that lay on the eastern side of Judd Street. The young tearaway who'd been molesting my Emmy lived with his mum and dad and his big brother in rooms in the Peabody Buildings that occupied a long stretch of the street. I also knew that the little sod's older brother, a real hard nut, had just come out of Brixton. This didn't worry us; if things got nasty, so be it.

We made our way across the dismal courtyard, past playing kids, and headed for the block where I knew that the Robinson family lived.

I bangs on the door, Roscoe hangs back in the shadows, the mother opens the door and I tell her that I'd like a word with her husband. She goes back in and her place is taken by the dad of the family. I tell him who I am and why I'm here and I would like to have a quiet word with the boy.

As expected, I'm told to 'F— off', then the father is joined by the big brother. At the same time Roscoe steps forward. Roscoe, with his big bent Jewish conk, was no small boy and in this new coat of his he looked enormous. Roscoe's appearance on the dark landing cooled the situation. 'You tell your kid to behave himself,' I said to the father, completely ignoring the brother, 'because if my little sister tells me that he's been messing about again I'll tan 'is arse so that 'e won't sit down for a week. I'm talking family here, you understand that?' The father hesitated but finally agreed that I was protecting my sister and understood that it was family. 'I'll tell 'im.' 'That's it, then, I'm satisfied,' I said and me and Roscoe walked back down the stairs, only to be followed by the big brother and a mate of his who had been attracted by the noise of the small altercation. It was obvious that this bruiser meant business. I glanced at Roscoe who just shrugged his shoulders. Then, suddenly, as we went out through the door the big brother stepped right in front of me. Instantly I swung a right to his gut and followed up with a left which landed smack between his eyes. Bull's-eye: the brother went down like a sack of coal, not out but quite incapable of taking any further interest in our departure. I bent down and whispered in the lad's ear: 'Family, mate, you ought to know the drill', and off we went back out into Herbrand Street. 'Blimey, Vic, why didn't you hit that bloke up at the gym like that?' 'I've been lugging hundredweight sacks of spuds all day since then, and, anyway, like the man said, he should learn to keep 'is guard up.' I thanked Roscoe and went to tell Emmy that I didn't think she would be troubled by the Robinson boy again, but, if she was, she must let me know. Then I went back into the kitchen to get my few hours kip before another day at the Garden.

Dear little Emmy had been causing me some grief, telling Mum that me and my girl Peggy wasn't in love any more. Mum said to me, 'I'm not surprised, knocking about with all those layabouts from Sidmouth Street. Every one of them will end up in prison. What nice girl would want to be seen dead with the likes of you lot?' In vain I pleaded the good points of the lads who I called my mates. It cut no ice with Mum. Then I tried another tack.

'Mum, why do I want to waste my time walking around with girls? Somehow I've got to earn a fortune so as you ain't got to keep slaving. And I got to keep an eye on Emmy. I ain't got no time for other women.' Mum's riposte to this was: 'What's the matter with you, Victor? You're getting on for eighteen. Don't you feel it's time to find yourself a nice girl, start saving up and things like that? You're getting a real big boy now, you carn't stay here with me and Emmy much longer, surely you realise that?' Then I said, 'I do think about these things but I ain't going to cart a girl around just for the sake of it.' I went on in the same vein. I wanted to tell her that if I did ever get married and have kids I wouldn't do what my father had done, but I stopped short of that, knowing full well it would bring back memories and hurt her.

36

Trouble in the Garden

Probably the most exciting event in the opening months of 1937 was the great flood. It was estimated that the Thames rose thirteen feet above its normal maximum. The Market almost came to a standstill. The produce continued to be delivered by the railways and was piling up in the streets all around the Garden and halfway up Drury Lane, causing utter chaos. This state of affairs went on for about a week before the authorities finally cleared the debris and the trade started moving freely again. The whole Embankment was under water from Lambeth to the Tower and beyond.

The Sabinis made one last bid for power with an American-style attempt to muscle in on a protection racket involving the smaller fruit firms that had premises to the south of the Garden. Four Sabini brothers arrived in London from New York and were living with the other members of the family in Millman Street which became their headquarters. It seemed that a small group of the gang had threatened serious violence to any of the stallholders who refused to pay up, whereupon they had been set on by a group of porters with their sack hooks. The rumour was that two members of the Sabinis ended up in potato sacks and were dropped in the river, never to be seen again.

Traders on the north side of the Garden didn't know what had happened until the law started coming around with pictures of various individuals, and asking if anyone had set eyes on them in the last week. Of course nobody would let on, even if they had.

The gang never showed their faces in the Garden again and the police, no doubt concluding that discretion was the better part of valour, let the whole thing drop.

Then something else happened. A small group of Mosley's lot set up a platform almost on the edge of the Garden itself where it joins Long Acre and, inevitably, a fight broke out between the porters and the Blackshirts. This was the first time since I started working for Maisie that I had seen violence in the Garden. This was a real bust-up and in no time the law was around in force rounding up the porters who had been knocking the Blackshirts about. Then up comes a police car out of which gets a senior copper with all this silver braid round his cap to prove it. I recognised him as one of the regulars who I used to pass Abe's envelopes to. I left Maisie's side, went up to him and said, 'Hello, mate, must be over a year since we last met.' I could see he recognised me and knew what I meant. He stared at me for a second, saying nothing, then he walked over to the luckless porters who were expecting to end the day in the cells at Bow Street nick. He told his constables to let them go. He was exercising clemency; no further action was necessary.

Maisie saw all this and said, 'I always knew you had a dark past, Victor, but I'm not going to poke my nose in.' She never mentioned the incident again.

37

Frankie's Café

One Saturday afternoon, I was sitting in Frankie's café in Gray's Inn Road with Roscoe and a couple of his mates. There was a bloke sitting in the café all on his lonesome. Toby, who was one of Rozzie's mates, went over to Frankie and asked him if he knew the lad. No, Frankie said that the bloke has been in a couple of times but he didn't know anything about him. Toby went and sat down opposite this unknown. 'Whatcha, mate, you new round 'ere?' Instead of looking annoyed at this direct approach, he told Toby that his parents had just arrived in the country and he didn't know anyone but that he'd learnt some English at school.

The long and short of it was that in no time he was sitting down with us and had accepted our invitation to come up to Harry's gym for a couple of hours. He told us he lived in Harrison Street and it was better than where he came from, so we assumed that he must have come from a right dump. We couldn't pronounce his name so Toby, who'd taken to the kid, called him Mickey because his name started with an 'M'.

When we arrived at Harry's one of the lads came over. 'Care for a couple of rounds, Vic?' I knew that this wasn't going to be serious stuff so I said I was OK for a little knockabout. Rozzie and the other three lads pulled up chairs to watch the fun, which ended with blood streaming down the front of my vest. We two warriors went four good rounds before calling it a day. Meanwhile, the new lad, Mickey, demonstrated his agility by shinning up the ropes that hung from the ceiling. The speed with which the lad climbed to the top was unbelievable. Everybody was watching him and I know that they were all thinking, 'Wonder what he's like up a drainpipe?' The bloke was by now the centre of attraction and agreed to try his luck with one of the local lightweights. The bundle began and there was no doubt about it, the kid was quick but not quick enough. He stopped a left-hander, got dumped on the canvas and that was the end of that. Everyone gave him a slap on the back.

On the tram back home the kid told us that his mother and father had come to England because the local police where he came from had started rounding up all of his dad's mates and that once they disappeared they were never seen again. His dad had said that England was the only country in the world where people could find refuge. We didn't have a clue what he was talking about and, as he seemed to be a decent lad, Toby told him to keep his prowess as a climber to himself. Mickey never really became one of us but now and again he would join up with us. I don't know what eventually became of him or even where he came from. I guess it was Germany.

Frankie's café had been our unofficial headquarters and meeting place for the last three years. On one occasion about half a dozen of us were sitting round playing a few hands of solo when in came none other than the Bear, towing along behind him a young copper who none of us had seen before.

We greeted the Bear – 'Afternoon, Mr Thomas' – all very respectful like. 'Wanna cup of splosh?' 'Only passing by,' said the Bear, 'see what mischief you lot are up to these days. And you, young Victor, what you doing round 'ere, Kenton Street too good for you?' Dusty butted in, 'You ain't come round 'ere for nuffink, sergeant, what yer looking for? We're all clean.' The Bear came back, looking straight at me. 'I don't know what this one's involved with at the moment and I'm aware none of you are on the thieve, but it's only luck that you and yer old man' (now he looked straight at Roscoe) 'ain't been run in and that goes for all three of you.

'Anyway, in case you don't know, in the last month there's been three cases of rape around the Cross. As far as we know there are two men involved and we reckon they're outsiders. So far it's been kept out of the papers, you lot 'eard anything?' 'News to us,' said Roscoe, 'but I will tell you this, sergeant, if you don't know already, if we ever get our hands on them, those bastards are lumbered. By the time you get your 'ands on them they will probably be minus their dicks. And who's this new bloke you're trotting around wiv?' Roscoe pointed to the shiny new member of our local constabulary. 'We got some new recruits and a new Super and he wants to make a name for himself so don't tell me you ain't been warned.'

With that, one of the few coppers we trusted stalked out into the sunshine.

Within three weeks the two rapists had been cornered up the top of Penton Street by a group from the Collier Street mob. One of the victims had been the sister of the lot from round the back of Millman Street. The Collier Street lot had sent word to the Millman Street lads that they should feel free to come and collect the two blokes. A couple of the Millman hard men dragged the two unfortunates off in a car and later on threw them out on to the steps of Judd Street nick minus their dicks and in a very bloody state. Although everybody knew the names of the two hard men, they were never grassed up to the police.

38

The Loss of Sammy and Maisie

'Tell yer what,' I said to Rozzie one day. 'How do you feel about 'aving a meal in a decent restaurant?' Rozzie agreed that it would make a change and so I took him round to Percy Street to the restaurant run by Ron's dad. 'Haven't seen you for a few weeks, Vic,' said Ron. I explained it was the market job and the hours I had to work: straight to kip by nine at the latest, up at two and into the market by three. 'It's real graft but the money is good. As for this bloke here,' I nodded to Roscoe, 'I ain't got a clue what 'e does for a living but 'e was the clarinet player in the band I told you about.' Ron suddenly perked up a bit. I knew what he was thinking: Roscoe might be a useful addition to our duo. Then Roscoe chimed in, 'I dropped that, Vic, I'm on the guitar now.' Then Ron asked, 'Ever heard of Django Reinhardt, mate?' It turned out that Roscoe's only source of musical inspiration was Roy Rodgers, 'the Singing Cowboy'. The gleam that I had seen in Ron's eyes faded, and I saw the promise of a free meal sliding away, so I chipped in, 'I reckon the three of us ought to give it a try, get together for a couple of hours. Lend Rozzie the record and let him do a bit of practice.' 'Better than that,' said Ron, 'I'll bring the machine down and we can 'ave a listen while we're eating.' Ron's eyes are lighting up again; if only we could get a halfway decent guitar and bass player we might make a go of it, although Ron must have known that his future was bound up with the café. Ron went to get the player and Rozzie sat in silence, looking a bit depressed.

'Whatsamatter, Roz? You look as if the world's coming to an end.' 'Tell yer what, Vic, I've put some skirt up the spout, and I'm expecting a visit any day soon.' 'What yer mean? Wiv a shotgun?' 'Could be,' said Roz, 'she's the sister of one of that Somers Town lot.' 'I always thought your mum said you had to marry "a nice little Jewish girl". You sure it's yours?' ''Fraid so,' said Roz, 'got to be honest about it, all mine.' 'Blimey.' Rozzie was almost the same age as me, heading for eighteen; the most I'd ever achieved was a few desperate kisses and a fumbling feel with my lost love Peggy, while my mate Roz had put one away in the oven.

Ron heard this and gave his solution to the problem. 'Only one fing to do, Rozzie; join the army and get posted somewhere out of the way.' 'Carn't do that, I've already thought about it. I can't join up until I'm eighteen and the thing will be out by then.'

There's no doubt about it, poor Rozzie was in dead trouble. At that moment Ron's mum brought up the grub, and his dad put our beloved Hot Club on the turntable. 'Get an earful of that, Roz, and tell us if you can do something like it, and remember that geyser who's playing the guitar has two broken fingers.'

It was quite obvious from the start that the genius of Stéphane and company didn't do anything for Rozzie. 'Is that wot they call jazz? Then, nah, don't care for that.' My attempt to enrol Roscoe into our twosome had failed at the first hurdle. Suddenly, as if let out of a cage, Ron blurted out, 'I can't hold back any more, Roscoe, how on earth did you get that bent conk? It's got to be the ugliest conk I've ever seen.' Talk about calling a spade a spade; I had visions of Ron getting flattened against the wall, but, no, Roscoe laughed it off. 'I tell yer wot, Ron, if you're out to catch a bird it's not the conk wot matters.' Roscoe being the type of bloke who didn't give a cuss for anyone hadn't lowered his voice and the punters in the café were roaring with laughter at what was being said. I'm sure that Ron got a talking to from his mum after we left. 'Who's that rough lot you're mixing with? And don't forget we expect you to marry a nice Italian girl, one that goes to church regularly.' Neither Roscoe nor I could come up with a solution to the problem of the impending 'visit'.

I was slowly losing interest in the job at the Garden, prob- ably because of the lack of social contact. What stopped me leaving were my feelings of loyalty to Maisie and Sammy. They had taken me on and broken the unwritten code of the market: everything was family, no entrance to outsiders. Not that there was any hostility to me; it was accepted that I was doing my bit to keep Maisie's head above water; Sammy himself was by now unable to lift a sack of spuds.

Then one Monday morning, I'm not sure whether it was May or June, up came Bert with the horse and cart, but no Maisie or Sammy. There was another bloke with him who I'd never set eyes on before. Bert gave me the eye. 'Sammy's gone,' he said, 'passed away on Saturday night. Maisie will be here tomorrow. We've got to do our best to keep the customers happy. Solly here will give a hand but he knows nuffink about the business.' Bert went off to have a chat with one of the other firms a little way down the road. After a bit a woman came up and said she's going to look after Maisie's side of the business and we must do what she said. Everyone set to with a will and by ten thirty Bert was back with the wagon and the shutters were going up. That was the only day I never had a breakfast. I wouldn't have been able to get it down if I had been offered one. All through the morning men and women had come up to offer their condolences and to give a hand if necessary. It was a great show of strength and unity on the part of the market people.

Maisie, Bert and this other chap turned up the next morning. The funeral had been arranged for the following Sunday so as not to interfere with the market trade. Maisie told me it was going to be held at a synagogue in Bethnal Green and I was welcome to come. But I decide that this was a highly religious affair, the family in their dozens would be in attendance, and it wasn't the place for a gentile like me. I told Maisie this and she put her head on my shoulders and wept away like a waterfall.

Later Maisie broke the news that she had decided there was no way she could carry on without her Sammy so she was going to sell up. There would be work for me until such time that somebody else took over the business, which should be in about three weeks. Then Maisie said, 'I'll see you're taken care of when I go, but I have to tell you, Victor, that you won't be taken on by whoever buys the firm, it's all Jewboys 'ere. I know you understand, Victor, you know the score.' 'That's OK, Maisie, I can take care of myself and I do know the score, so no ill feelings on my part.' 'We'll all go down the boozer and get sloshed before we go, Victor – go out wiv a bang, sort of.'

Maisie was true to her word. I invited Roscoe to the beer-up and for the first time in my young life got pissed as a newt. Rozzie and me staggered home completely sozzled.

The job held on for another three weeks and then Maisie told me that the Saturday coming would be our last day of business. She also told me that she had tried to get me another job but that she didn't have much say in the matter. 'I'll see you all right, Victor, you've been a great help to us.' So we carried on and each day seemed to get gloomier than the last. Finally, on the Saturday morning, we put up the shutters for the last time and Maisie made a cuppa on the little stove in the corner of the shop. Then she opened a box of nice pastries, and her eyes were wet with tears. I reckoned she would never get over the loss of her Sammy and I remembered my own mum with her eyes streaming as she sat on those dark winter nights bewildered and hurting at the loss of her Eddy. It was these two women, neither of whom knew each other, who taught me that it is the women who suffer most from the ups and downs of life.

Maisie gave me a hug and then a lecture. 'Victor, you listen to me, you've the makings of a good boy, but at your age you should be thinking of your future. Who was that scruffy Jewboy you brought along with you the other night?' 'That was my mate Roscoe, he's all right.' 'All right my foot,' said Maisie. 'Look at 'is 'ands the next time you meet up wiv 'im, never done a day's work in 'is life. Looks like a crook to me. 'E must be breaking 'is poor muvver's 'eart. Yer got to make somefink of yerself, Victor. Don't forget us, yer know where we live', and with that she shoved an envelope in my hand. 'It's something for yer to put in the Post Office. It's not a free gift, Victor, you've earned every penny, now get along wiv yer, you're breaking me poor Jewish heart.'

I had feelings within me that are hard to describe. I wanted this woman who was not my mother to put her arms about me. I wanted her to know that if she needed support then I would be on hand to give it, in the same way that I used to feel when our mum had her dark moments thinking about our dad.

And that was the last I saw of Maisie. The envelope contained one hundred pounds in fivers, an enormous sum, and a letter explaining to any future employer how lucky they were to have me applying for a job. I held on to the money until Monday when I went round the local post office and deposited the whole lot in a savings account which paid an interest rate of two and a half per cent – sixpence in the pound. I opened the account in my mother's name. That evening when she came home from work I told her about the money Maisie had given me and gave her the book with the hundred pounds written in and officially stamped. My mum had never had so much money in her life. Suddenly, just like Maisie, she burst into a flood of tears.

The loss of Sammy and Maisie affected me more than I cared to admit. I really felt as if Maisie was my second mother. Now they were gone and there was nothing to take their place. I used to think about what it was like to be Jewish, but then Rozzie was a Jewboy and he and his dad had nothing in common with Sammy. I used to lie in bed thinking about the words of advice that Maisie had given me and went on wondering if I really was the son she never had and what it would have been like to have Sammy as my dad. One evening, in a fit of self-pity, I told my mum about these troubling thoughts. She told me, 'The world is full of good people', and I should consider myself lucky to have found Sammy and Maisie and that she was going to the minister to offer up a prayer for the pair of them. Mum added that for me to be thinking such things showed that I was at last growing up. She said that all I had to do now was to 'stop going around with that rough lot from where we used to live'.

39

Bookie's Runner

For a week I mooched around like a fish out of water. I went up to the labour to suss what was on offer and quickly realised that if I wanted a worthwhile job I wasn't going to get it there. Finally, I went and found Roscoe who was sitting in the usual café with his customary bunch of mates. Once we got through the opening formalities and mickey taking he said, 'Got anuvver job yet, Vic?' 'Nope, still looking.' One of Roscoe's mates chipped in: 'About time yer packed up slinging them sacks about and missing all the fun in the evenings. Done yer a good turn, the old man kicking the bucket like that.' Roscoe, not wanting a flare up in the café, told his mate to shut 'is gob or e'd shut it for 'im. 'The old lady gave me a 'undred quid when I left. As a matter of interest, Roscoe, she reckoned you was probably a right crook, said she thought that you'd never done a day's work in yer life. Well, I managed to half convince her that you wasn't a crook but I must admit to the fact that I've never heard tell of any job yer may of 'ad.'

Roscoe didn't seem at all put out by the way the conversation was going. 'That's because it's not in my interest to advertise the way I earn me dosh. You've never asked, I've never told, and furthermore I say nuffink more than I 'ave to. But I tell yer this, Vic, if yer ever want to earn a couple of bob the easy way, not thieving or anyfink like that, I'll show yer the ropes. My word will get yer in.' I sat down at the table and the other couple of lads went on discussing what they had been discussing before I came in — the likely winners and also-rans of the afternoon's sporting calendar.

'Ever do the 'orses or the dogs?' said Roscoe. 'Don't know nuffink about them,' I said. 'Ain't yer ever 'ad a bet then?' said one of Rozzie's mates. 'Wouldn't know the first thing about it.' Then Roscoe upped and said he'd got to get away. 'Fings to see to,' he said. 'Come round tonight, Vic, we'll go down the Albion and 'ave a pint, I got business down there so I'll be in there till nine, OK, Vic? Might give yer a few ideas.' After that I left the café and sauntered down to Percy Street looking for Ron but he was out so I had a coffee and made my way to my mum's place of work in Bridle Lane. I'd do what I used to do a long time ago: walk home with my mum.

Later that evening I was sitting in the Albion, a beer house just off the Pentonville Road. It was known as a beer house because it didn't sell spirits. You could have what you liked as long as it was beer, and Whitbread's Best at that. Roscoe showed up around six thirty and, ignoring me, went round the tables collecting money and giving out little chits of paper. When he'd got all that sorted he came over. 'That's the opener for the dogs at Catford,' he said. The penny dropped.

So that was what my mate Roscoe was into: he was a book-ie's runner.

'You can 'ave a go, Vic. The only fing, you got to keep yer mouth shut, yer customers will know yer, that's all, come on, I got another three pubs to do tonight.'

So off we went on a working pub crawl. By the end of the evening I'd begun to get the hang of things. 'The most important fing, Vic, is to keep yer eyes open for the law, and make sure you're never followed on the way back to me dad.' 'What about if they hit a winner?' 'You got it right first time, Vic, "if" is the magic word. You take the winnings round the next night, so you're always loaded with cash. If you want to give it a go I'll put a word in wiv the old man, but I tell yer straight, if yer ain't quick enough, the rozzers will nab yer. They fine yer a fiver every time you go up in front of the beak, and he'll tell you he's going to be lenient if you tell the court the name of the bookie. Naturally you don't know nuffink, you always pass the bets on to some geezer on the corner of the street, they know the score, everyone knows the score, not a problem, if you're quick you can make a fiver a week.' With that mouthful I now knew the ins and outs of the illegal gambling trade and how Roz could afford all the new gear he was always wearing. A fiver a week? He was almost a millionaire. 'I'll follow you around for a couple of days, Roz, make sure I know the drill.' With that we went our different ways for what was left of the night. After he'd gone I realised that I hadn't asked him how he was getting on with the other little problem of the bird with the bump on her belly, but Roscoe hadn't appeared to be unduly worried.

40

Back with Eddie Again

I had been involved with some shady characters in the last couple of years – no more than might be expected, considering the area I was growing up in – but did I really want to follow the road that Roscoe was offering? I thought of Maisie and the hundred quid she had given me. A hundred quid was a fortune and yet she must have had enough faith in me to give me that much. I knew that somehow I had to get a worthwhile job, but that was easier said than done.

The next morning I went down to Chiswick to see if I could get any joy from Eddie Wilson. I just couldn't see him and his mate working for anybody else. He must have something going.

Eddie lived in a small house off Chiswick High Road. When I knocked on the door I was greeted by his missus. 'Hello, Victor, you've grown a bit, come in and 'ave a cup of tea, I suppose you've come down to see Eddie. What about a nice bacon sandwich?' I started to cheer up. If his missus was so happy, maybe Eddie was earning again.

'I've come down to see if Eddie can find me something interesting like what we used to do.' 'Well, I don't know much about Eddie's business, he rented a garage out last week but what he's doing with it for the life of me I don't know. I do know that he hasn't given me any housekeeping money for the last couple of weeks but knowing him something will turn up.' My hopes that had been rising with each mouthful of the lovely bacon sandwich plummeted to zero. 'Why don't you nip round the corner and see what he's up to?'

Wherever there is a railway line running through a town or city so also will there be these rows upon rows of arches and in the arches you will find all manner of workshops. It was one such workshop that Eddie was renting.

I found Eddie on his lonesome knee, up to his waist in old pipework, bits of rusty metal and other debris. 'Bloody hell, Vic, you're the last bloke I expected to see. What's up?' I told him the sorry tale and of my determination to make millions before I reached twenty-one. 'I've been slaving all my life, Vic and I 'avn't got a brass farthing to show for it. I got offered this place cheap so I'm going to try to get a little business going, repairs and maybe the odd renovation. I've got a few contacts, anything is better than working for wages.' This was the old governor that I understood. 'Tell you what, Eddie, take me on and start paying me when you start earning.' 'You mean you're willing to work for nix?' 'I've just been round your house and your missus done me a lovely bacon roll, if she can keep me from starving during the day I'm willing to stay.' 'Vic, we'll be up and running by next Monday, we clear all the rubbish out today and tomorrow we

clean down the walls and get my old machinery in. Don't
worry, I'll 'ave you earning in a couple of weeks. Let's go
down the café and 'ave a meal before we get stuck in.' Which
we did. I wasn't worried about the money. I was back with
Eddie and in no time we'd be up to all the old tricks producing little sports cars out of Austin Sevens and Morris Eights
and cheap old Fords. I knew that Eddie wasn't exactly what
you would call straight, and I knew that some of the old
tricks would include grinding off engine registration numbers
and such like. The law would take a dim view of this, I knew
that, but Eddie wasn't a bad man. He didn't go around hitting
people. He sailed close to the wind, but a lot of people did
that just to survive. As far as I was concerned it was honest
work for a slightly dishonest governor.

The little jobs started to come in: engine stripdowns and
the like, welding and brazing jobs, enough to keep us ticking
over. Eddie supplied the technical know-how and me the
brute force. He liked the way he could tell me what to do
and how to do it. If he was working with someone a bit older
and better versed in the trade he wouldn't have been able to
do this, but with me he had it all his own way, which was fine
by me. Once again I was earning money and enjoying life in
the process.

One day Eddie's old mate Charlie the panel beater joined
the firm and it looked like, for Eddie, all was well with the
world. I thought Eddie and his mate were top of the class. I
met up with Roscoe a week after I started with Eddie and
told him about my return to the motor trade. Rozzie wasn't
at all put out by my decision to turn down his offer; he was

more concerned by what he called the 'rantings' of his dad. Apparently there was going to be another war and it could start any day now. His dad had been to a meeting called by the local synagogue and the Rabbi had given his audience a lecture on what was happening in Germany now that this bloke Hitler had settled in. Half the population was in the nick and the other half were slaving their heads off making tanks, aeroplanes and battleships. People were being shot in the streets and anyone who complained was strung up. 'That's what the Rabbi told us and if you can't believe the Rabbi then who can you believe?' You went to work, got some dosh and after giving some to your mum, spent the rest on yourself. That was my world. War sounded exciting, though.

I said as much to Eddie who replied that if the Germans carried on the way they are doing then it was true we would end up at war with them. 'How much do they pay yer for going to war then, Eddie?' Eddie looked at me as if he couldn't believe I was so stupid. 'Don't pay nothing, Vicky boy, and most likely you'll get yourself killed. There's a rule that says never volunteer for anything, especially wars.'

What really set me thinking was when our mum came home one night from work and announced that the firm had another big contract for military hats. 'Like Uncle Frank makes at his firm and we got enough work for the next three years.' Uncle Frank was Mum's elder brother and he was a cutter at Ayres and Smith, this firm in Lexington Street that specialised in military hats for the higher ranks, both army and navy. 'Do you think there's going to be another war, Mum?' 'Not on your life, Victor, there was too many killed in the last one, nobody would be so daft as to start all that again.' That was the view and wisdom of my mother who had lost two of her brothers in the last lot. Rozzie's dad was wrong. I thought he must be a nutcase.

I would have liked to have asked Sammy and Maisie what they thought but Sammy was gone and I hadn't seen Maisie since we packed up at the market. I wanted to take a trip to Bethnal Green and have a chat with her but I never did. I wondered whether Maisie missed me as much as I missed her.

On the whole Eddie ran the business as an ordinary garage; a customer brought in a car for repair, we fixed it, whatever it was, and the punter would leave satisfied with a job well done. Eddie couldn't do the resprays in the workshop, because every time a train went overhead everything got smothered in dust.

Every now and then a car was brought in, the engine lifted out and cleaned. At which point Eddie or Charlie set about removing any distinguishing numbers or metal tags; anything that could give the game away was removed or ground out. By the time the three of us had completed our various jobs the car bore little resemblance to the vehicle that had entered the garage a few days before. It turned out this was all done for a couple of big garages that had put up the money for Eddie to rent the workshop. Who the blokes were earning the real money out of these cars we never knew, and we never asked. That was the deal and we all knew the score.

Like the last time I had worked for Eddie all the spares that we bought were bent, but then three-quarters of the second-hand car markets in London were bent. The source of the stolen accessories was the railway goods depot at Somers Town. Goods made in Birmingham and the Midlands in general ended up there awaiting distribution, or, in our case, redistribution from the back of a lorry.

One day I rode into the yard to find Eddie and Charlie having a real go at each other, not fighting or anything like that, but they were having words and this was no normal difference of opinion. Charlie said, 'Go down the café, Vic, come back in an hour.' I looked at Eddie and he nodded. When I came back the two of them said to me, 'Vic, we've decided and what we're going to say to you is in your own interest; you've got to get out. We don't want you around any more.'

The previous night Charlie had been visited by the law. A lad handling the stolen goods had been picked up and named our garage as one of the receivers. Charlie, who had form, was visited first. Eddie expected his turn to come at any moment. They were piling the incriminating evidence into Charlie's little Morris van. 'If you stay here, Vic, and we go down, the chances are you'll come along, too. Best for you to make yourself scarce.' With that Eddie pulls out a wad of notes, puts them in an envelope along with my cards. 'That's it then, Eddie?' 'Sorry, son, but you're old enough to know the score, you've been around.' They both give me a slap on the shoulder and I'm off, another job down the drain.

Before I left the garage Charlie told me it had been the Frazer Nash that was the cause of the trouble.

The Frazer had arrived at the garage in a covered van about a month before. We had real trouble unloading it. All we had were a couple of twelve-foot scaffolding boards on which we managed to wheel the beast down from the van to ground level. There were only two cars of the thirties that used a chain drive for the transmission; one was a Jowett and the other, much more sophiscated and sought after, was the Frazer Nash, a completely British car. The one we had unloaded was the most sought after of them all, a two-year-old TT Sports Replica. The owner had returned it to the dealer in Great Portland Street because it had developed a bad case of rust in the chassis, a common problem in cars of that period. Eddie was known in the London trade as being a Frazer Nash expert. He had been visiting the Frazer Nash dealer in Great Portland Street when he first invited me to work for him. I imagine he had promised the dealer he could repair this car so it would be good as new.

We hoisted it on a set of blocks and stripped it down to its last nut and bolt. We found the rust had eaten right through the metal. It was impossible to weld. Eddie needed a new chassis and that was a problem: Frazer Nash wouldn't provide a chassis on its own. You had to order it with a complete body. The company didn't want it getting about that the chassis were vulnerable to rust. The dealer had told Eddie not to worry, he'd sort it out.

My first task was to clean the whole thing up while Charlie got busy knocking out the dents in the bodywork and Eddie stripped the engine down. Then Eddie balanced all the moving parts and I got myself smothered in the dark red rouge paste that we used to polish all the steel parts like the piston rods, cam followers and tappets. They all had to be brought up to a mirror finish, which I did with the aid of an old lathe that took up half the shop. The mirror finish wasn't just for show; it served two purposes, one to show up any fractures and two to allow the oil to flow freely through the engine. Eddie knew his stuff all right.

Within a couple of weeks the same delivery van that had brought in the motor in the first place turned up with the new chassis and naturally I get the job of cleaning it up. Lo and behold, this so-called spare chassis had got a registration number on it. So Charlie took it off and replaced it with the number from the old chassis. The new plate was cut up and thrown away. When the car was finally rolled out of the arches the delighted client remarked, 'better than new'.

It was a trail of Frazer Nash spare parts that had suddenly surfaced on the Warren Street and Great Portland Street markets that led the law to Eddie's front door.

There was no way that Eddie or anyone else in the scam was going to drop names. He was never going to tell anyone where the chassis had ended up. To keep the law from further prodding, Eddie and Charlie must have agreed to do a bit of time, knowing full well that they would eventually be rewarded by the criminal syndicates that ran these stolen car rackets. It was the name of the game. Everyone understood the rules.

41

Granddad Reflects

It was the weekend that I had parted company with Eddie, a Saturday afternoon, and it was unusually warm and sunny for the time of the year. Out in the backyard at Kenton Street I was giving my grandfather a hand clearing the mountains of junk that had accumulated in the shed that ran along the length of the backyard. My grandmother called it the back garden on account of the small flower patch that she managed to keep alive and in bloom. To everyone else it was 'the yard', the place where we kept the dustbins and other rubbish, an area crisscrossed with clothes lines.

'Your dad built this shed for us when he was courting your mother.' Grandfather told me this as if it was a vital part of my education. 'What do you know about him, Granddad, and why do you think he left our mum?' Grandfather didn't answer this question right away but carried on cutting up the lengths of lead water piping that he was hoping he could get me to trundle round to the local scrapyard.

'He was a decent enough chap. He thought the world of your mum. He was a damn good plumber into the bargain, he could turn 'is 'and to anything, reminded me and your gran of our Jack, two of a kind they were. You know that Jack was your mum's brother, got gassed in sixteen, came 'ome and got sent out again. He was killed at Passchendaele. Your dad went right through the war, must 'ave been under-age when he enlisted but 'e was a tall chap, plenty of meat on 'im, that's 'ow 'e got in, collected a piece of shrapnel in 'is leg, came 'ome. Because of 'is leg they shoved him in the Royal Engineers, that's how he learnt about the plumbing, when 'e joined he was in the Royal Fusiliers, a machine-gun mob. He met your mum when he was in the infirmary at Richmond and your mum was in the Church Army helping out at the hospitals.' 'If you thought he wasn't so bad why do you think he upped and went?' By now Grandfather was sitting in an old wicker chair that he kept in the shed. He answered the question slowly and with some thought. 'Who can tell, Victor? I know your grandmother will never forgive him. For me, I've seen what war does to men, seen it meself, I 'ave. My opinion is that 'e's a goner – dead and gorn. We traced his name to a ship that was going to Australia, an immigrant boat, that's as far as we got. Remember this, Victor, never condemn anyone till you know the facts. Your mum and dad were married at St Pancras Church. None of his family turned up for the wedding. That alone must 'ave caused 'im some pain.' This little talk with my grandfather reminded me of the time my dad had taken me to a football match and told me always to love my mum.

42

Soldier Boy

A month later, driven by curiosity, I cycled down to Eddie's house and his wife told me the sorry tale. The pair of them, Eddie and Charlie, went down for six months each for handling stolen goods. She thought Charlie had been lucky to get off so lightly seeing as he had previous form. Why was it that I always ended up with the villains? I knew you never earned a real wage working in a factory. I'd tried it. I didn't have the mentality that would allow me to punch a card every morning and do the same boring job, day in and day out. But that was all very well; I was nearly eighteen and had to earn some money.

That night I was in the café discussing this tale of woe with Rozzie. 'Yeah, the clowns went and got themselves nicked,' I said.

Rozzie gave his mates the eye and let out a sort of croaking laugh. 'Didn't you 'ear about us, then? Course you wouldn't, you ain't been around for weeks. The old man got nabbed and we only got away wiv it by the skin of our teeth.' ''E's not inside, is 'e?' I asked. 'No, the beak said 'e was too old, fined 'im two 'undred quid. 'E says 'e's skint now but I don't believe 'im, not my old man, 'e's bound to 'ave some stashed away under the bed.'

'What you doing now, then?' 'Same as you, Vic, casting me peepers around, no joy in being skint.'

The following day Roscoe's brother turned up with four tickets for the Ring at Blackfriars. Roscoe's pride and joy, Harry Mizler, was in one bout and, to top it all off, Tommy Hyams of King's Cross was on the same bill. 'F— the world, let's go and see a good bundle.' Harry Mizler won on a knockout. Tommy, who was considered to be on the way out, lost on points, and a good time was had by all.

Another week went by and still no job. I hadn't seen Roscoe since our night at the Ring. The next day was 15 October, my eighteenth birthday.

I climbed out of bed early the next morning, saw Emmy off to school and then set off to see what I could find. It wasn't a good day for walking the streets but I made it down to Drury Lane and eventually to Horse Guards Parade, where the redcoats on their horses were doing their daily stint. I was in a dream world drifting along, not connected to anything, when, suddenly, I got tapped on the shoulder. 'You all right, son?' says this giant of a man standing behind me. 'Yeah, I'm OK.' 'Care for a cup of tea and a bun, all on the 'ouse?' I must have nodded or something. 'Follow me then, let's see what we can grab hold of.' Then this figure, resplendent in his highly pressed uniform with his rows of medals glittering in the morning light, led me across Whitehall and into Great

Scotland Yard, under a darkened archway up the stairs. The doors shut with a whoosh, a strange sound that seemed to warn me that nothing would be the same again.

Twenty minutes later I emerged from the gothic mausoleum of a place with a railway warrant to Winchester. The rain was pelting down, a real miserable day. There was a poster on the wall opposite. It showed a soldier boy, lounging in the sunshine on some foreign shore, eyeing up the dusky maidens in their grass skirts. 'Join the Army and see the World' it said.

OK, I thought, might not be too bad. Give it a go, Vic.

43

Basic Training

The gas lamp out in the street was still flickering away when, after a sleepless night, I rose and gave myself a good rinse down. The water was freezing but that's what I wanted; today I would be leaving my family and they were quite unaware of the fact. Half of me wanted to stay but the other half wanted to go off into the unknown. I got up at the same time as Mother. I knew my mum enjoyed these occasions when I got up early and put the tea on. Sometimes on a Sunday I would bring her a cup before she got up. At times like that I felt that she wanted to give me a big kiss, but I was too old for that sort of thing; but on this particular morning I would have liked my mum to have given me that one last kiss. 'You going to look for a new job today, Victor?' 'Something like that, Mum, got to do something.' My mum finally put on her hat and coat and off she went on the walk to Bridle Lane and the sweatshop. Little Emmy was tarting herself up, getting ready for another day at school, although she wasn't so little any more and was fast learning the art of turning the local boys' heads. I become aware that I'm going to miss all of this.

I could hear my gran downstairs singing some song. I sat down at the table and I wrote out a short note to Mum, telling her not to worry about me and that I would write as soon as I got settled in. I could only manage about six lines and a dozen kisses. I folded up the notepaper and stuck it under the carriage clock which had pride of place on the mantelpiece. The clock had been a wedding present from one of her friends and my mum treasured it. She would see the note directly she entered the door. I remember writing that she was not to start crying as I was not leaving, just working away for a time.

I took the 68 bus to Waterloo and, armed with my free travel warrant, boarded the train that was going to take me to the unknown place called Winchester. Aboard the train, I had more second thoughts as I realised that with every clack, clack of the wheels I was getting further away from those I loved and respected. As the train sped through the suburbs of London I looked at the backs of the houses with their little gardens. In some of them I could see spades and wheelbarrows neatly stacked. Why didn't we have a nice house and garden instead of the rat hole I'd been born in? These thoughts filled my mind as the train carried me further and further away from King's Cross.

I remembered the time at the Shaftesbury when the head told me that big boys didn't cry. I pulled myself together and squared my shoulders as I arrived at Winchester. A sergeant was waiting for new arrivals and he tried to call me to order.

I felt like sticking my tongue out at him and giving him a bit of lip. Luckily I didn't attempt to assert my independence. Instead I formed up with the other six lads who had been on the train. The sergeant led us the short distance to the Rifle Brigade barracks which was perched on top of one of the hills that surround the city.

We were marched through the barrack gates, great iron things, and called to a halt outside the guardroom. Any ideas we had about a return to yesterday vanished as the soldier on guard shut the gates. There was a clang and a screech as the huge bolt was slid into place. We realised that this was it. The guardroom was spotless; anything made of metal glistened; the few pictures on the whitewashed walls were hung with mathematical precision. The wooden table was scrubbed to a surgical whiteness, and of course there were the soldiers themselves. Their trousers and jackets had creases that looked as if they could cut through steel. These men seemed to have been ironed and polished along with every other object in the room. Nothing was out of place. 'Wipe the dirt off them filthy shoes before any of you lot enter 'ere,' shouted a corporal.

After we had given our names and details the sergeant took us round to the stores where we were issued with our kit, which we had to sign for. Then we were led to a huge room which we were told would be our home for the next six months. 'All of yer git down to the showers and scrub off all that filthy muck you've accumulated in Civvy Street. You can throw those rags you're wearing into the bin, you won't need them any more. Boots and shoes as well, sling the lot. I want to see you all in the canteen at sixteen hundred hours sharp, scrubbed and looking sharp in all that expensive kit you've just been issued with. And in case you don't understand, all that shiny brass and scrubbed table and chairs is done by blokes who think they can take the mickey. You've got an hour, get to it.'

With much muttering about what we were going to do to this bloke if any of us met him in a dark alley, we made our way to the bathhouse and the freezing cold showers.

After the shower we discovered the shirt and vests didn't fit and the jackets were miles too narrow and the boots miles too big. On the stroke of four we all trooped down to the canteen, a real sorry looking lot. When he saw us the sergeant looked as if he was going to throw a fit but after a couple of seconds he saw the funny side of the situation. 'OK, lads, get this meal down yer guts and we'll be off to the stores again. Thirty minutes sharp.' He left us with half a dozen other blokes who had arrived the day before. We began to sort each other out, exchange names and other information about ourselves. We were a room full of strangers but didn't realise we were creating bonds that would tie us together for as long as life itself.

The sergeant turned up exactly thirty minutes later and in no time we were all dressed up in His Majesty's official finery with everything fitting like a glove. One item made me realise that I was in a different world – the boots. They weighed a ton and made the thin shoes I had arrived in, and which were now in the dustbin, seem like paper. The amazing thing was the speed with which I got used to them. Those boots were my initiation into the world of spit and polish.

Later, in the canteen the sergeant gave us a pep talk. 'Right you lot, listen to what I am going to say, and remember: in this regiment we only have room for men who can handle things in the proper manner. You get told once and once only. At six in the morning the bugler will be blasting yer eardrums out. That's when you crawl out of your stink pits. At six thirty you're down on the parade ground in your gym kit. And if you are late, God help you. Right, supper in the canteen at nineteen hundred hours. Dismiss.'

The next morning we were on the parade ground in the pouring rain, jumping up and down doing something called 'running on the spot', which seemed a waste of time to me. If you're going to run then you may as well run somewhere. By the time we were back in the barrack room some of the lads were beginning to think of ways to make a hasty exit from the predicament they had landed themselves in. Not me. I was beginning to enjoy myself. This was a challenge and I was ready to flex my muscles.

It took another two weeks before enough recruits arrived to make up the twenty-five men required for a training squad and another week of lectures before we held our first formal parade on the garrison square. We paraded complete with rifles (less firing pins), and by now we knew all too well that being a British soldier wasn't going to be a cakewalk.

There was one thing that linked my new world to my old. On the streets round King's Cross and Soho I had learnt to stand my ground and I would have to do the same thing on the parade ground in Winchester. The new intake wasn't short of lads who wanted to prove that they were top dog, and if you gave in to any of them you had had it. It took a fortnight to sort everything out. At the end of that time I knew who my mates were and would stand by them come what may

The Rifle Brigade was largely made up of Londoners. Your loyalties depended on which side of the River Thames you came from. Their were the 'northerners' and the 'southerners', each doing their best to outdo the other. This was encouraged by our masters. They reckoned the competition was good for us. If things got nasty the NCOs arranged for the two sides to meet in the gym and battle it out in the ring.

I didn't find it difficult to adapt to this new life; it was just a natural extension of the way I had always lived. The lads who found it difficult were the ones who had led a more sheltered life. There was one chap in the squad who had been forced to enlist by his father, a man who had once been a senior officer in the regiment. The boy had been to public school and had to start from the bottom. Luckily for him he was soon spotted by the colonel and whisked off to the safety of another establishment.

There was a sergeant who came from the battalion base at Tidworth to give us lectures, one of which emphasised the importance of looking on your section, platoon, company or indeed the whole battalion as one gang in which you all looked after each other, even if you hated the guts of the man standing next to you. 'That's the way this regiment fights its battles, that's why we have less losses than the brass button mobs.' ('Brass button mobs' was how we referred to the Guards regiments.)

Of the six of us who arrived on that train, four of us formed a strong friendship: Frankie Batt, Tommy Vine, Reggie Cole and me.

Tommy Vine got his early on at a place named Solum, on the very edge of the Libyan border. Frankie Batt was laid to rest at Alamein. Reggie made it to the end, all the way from the Western Desert, up through Italy and into France, almost into Germany itself, before the war ended. He breathed his last six years later of a dodgy heart condition.

I am the last survivor of that little group who offered themselves for service on 18 October 1937.

44

The End of the Beginning

After the first month of training we were given railway vouchers and a week's leave. Surprisingly, only about half the lads took the opportunity to go home. I spent quite a few nights wondering what sort of reception I would get. It had been nearly five weeks since I'd left. I had only written two letters home to my mum. She had answered them both, telling me not to worry. 'You never can tell, Victor, might be for the best, and you had to find your feet sometime.'

When I finally got home I made my way down the narrow stairs that led to our gran's kitchen. I noticed how dark and cramped it all was. 'Well, for the life of me, you have grown in such a short time, must be the food,' said my gran after she had given me a hug and a kiss. For the first time I noticed that my gran's hair was a silvery-grey. When Mum came home from work she was all smiles with the odd tear sliding down her cheeks. Then gran said, 'I want you to take us all to church on Sunday, and with you wearing that nice new uniform we are all going to be very proud of you, Victor.'

Mum went to great pains to assure me that she had more than enough to get by on and that the hundred pounds in the post office account had increased to a hundred and twenty. Brother John was still slaving away at the grocer's shop, and sister Emmy was going to try for grammar.

I was shocked to discover that my mate Roscoe was doing a spell in Wandsworth. I never found out what he had been done for, and I never found out what happened about the baby his girl was expecting. When I went round to his house his mum and dad were all over me. They were very upset about Roscoe's bit of trouble and said how much better it would have been if Roscoe had joined up with me. I agreed and said you can't have too many good mates when you're among strangers. I couldn't think of any of the squad who would want to mix it with me and Roscoe standing shoulder to shoulder.

I decided that I had to say goodbye to the lads who had been my mates for the last few years. I went round to Frankie's café where I was ribbed right, left and centre. We drank coffee and nattered away, just as we had always done, then I stood up and shook everybody's hands. On the way home I met Peg. I was walking back to Kenton Street through Cromer Street and there she was, standing talking with some of her friends, gently rocking a pram, like a real experienced mum. I stopped and our eyes met and the world around me went silent. I'm certain that Peg was going through the same emotions as I was. Then, in the same instant, the spell ended and in the politest possible way we said our hellos. 'You do look nice in your uniform, Vic.' 'You look top of the world yourself, Peg.' We both felt uncomfortable. I wanted more than anything to touch her hand, like in the old days. For the first time in my life I felt real guilt and I knew that I had lost something very precious. Whether she felt the same I shall never know. But we both knew the rules; you don't mess with someone else's girl, and anyway Peg was now married with a baby, so that was that. We had crossed a bridge and there was no going back. I was hurt but had no means of showing it. Next I went around to the restaurant in Percy Street and had a free meal with Ron and his mum and dad. They all showed genuine interest in my new career and asked me if I thought there was going to be a war. I had to admit I didn't have a clue. 'Your fiddle and music are still up in my room,' said Ron. I replied, 'You never know, Ron, you might break yours, so now you've got a spare.' That was the last I saw of Ron. It was a sad goodbye to the Stéphane Grappelli duets we used to play together.

On my last night I went for a walk with Grandfather to his club in Marylebone Lane. He took me into a pub and offered me a pint, but I only had a half. I didn't want to make an idiot of myself.

As we were supping up, my grandfather said, 'You wouldn't know this, Victor, but I was at Ladysmith when the Green Jackets were there. I suppose that your mob are still called Green Jackets? Take a tip from one who knows: the chief thing you need to learn now is survival. You've got yourself mixed up with a real death or glory lot, so watch yourself. If the Germans don't throw this Hitler out on his ear the bloody square heads will trample over Europe same as they did last time. I don't think you're going to have it very easy. So mark my words, watch yourself, remember that, and go with our blessing.'

My grandfather's words went in one ear and out of the other, but they all turned out to be true.

Next day I made my way back to my new life. I wasn't sad any more. I was a soldier boy now and there was nothing left for me in the streets that I had once called home. I walked away from King's Cross heading for Waterloo and the train back to the depot. My head was full of memories but I knew that my growing up was all done, all finished.

My apprenticeship was over.